RAMBLINGS OF A MIND & PULSATIONS OF A HEART

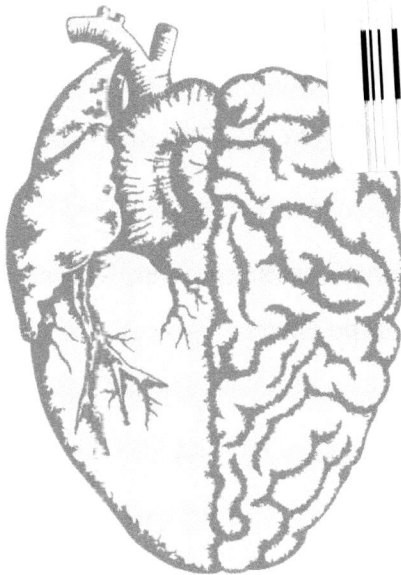

DR. VELON JOHN

© 2025 - Dr. Velon John

Published by Wakonté Books

www.wakontebooks.com

Paperback Edition published 2025

ISBN: 978-1-947923-11-9

All Scripture quotations, unless otherwise indicated, are taken from the King James Version of the Bible.

This book is dedicated to my deceased parents; my mother, **GRISELDA JOHN nee MAURICE,** who nurtured me, and my father, **WILLIAM FITZROY JOHN** who enlightened me.

ABOUT THE AUTHOR

VELON LEO JOHN who on a multiplicity of levels and in multifarious forms describes himself thus:

- A scrambler of words
- A mad leaper to a star
- An unfeathered biped
- With a soul that contradicts

"The concoction is madness," he declares.

Believing that to be sane in a world of insanity is itself insanity, Dr. John embraces the wisdom of his "madness" as a lens through which to view and interpret life.

Born in the village of Laborie on the island of Saint Lucia, Dr. John has distinguished himself by serving in all three arms of government: the Judiciary, the Legislature, and the Executive. He continues to practice law in his homeland, contributing to the nation he calls home.

Dr. John can be contacted via email at: velon.leo@gmail.com

AUTHOR'S NOTE

As you peruse these words and contemplate the sublime contradictions inherent in your relational posture, it may dawn upon you that the universe of your being is unfolding in ways that transcend the judgmental anticipation of yourself. These contradictions, far from obstacles, form the fundamental antithesis through which the authenticity of self can be realized.

If you can reconcile the unity of your person with the essential dualism and contradictions of self and conduct, you will, in time and within the context of your existence, discern a celestial vision—a truth shaped by the aspirations and insights of thousands of years. It is only by embracing this process of "becoming" that the deeper meaning of existence reveals itself.

As you engage in this exercise of thought, surrendering your cognitive innocence in the process, you will find yourself connected —despite the absence of my presence—to that which is abstruse yet real. This connection, though intangible, is sublime and emancipating, illuminating a path toward authenticity and profound self-awareness.

This book, however, is not a "credo" since our thinking is in a state of evolutionary flux embracing postures of enlightened skepticism and the ever-unfolding quest for understanding.

TABLE OF CONTENTS

ABOUT THE AUTHOR...ii

AUTHOR'S NOTE..iii

REFLECTIONS

LOVE 10

INFATUATION 29

FEMALE DIGNITY 33

VIRGINITY 36

A NOTION OF DEATH 60

SUICIDE 65

THE GENESIS OF EVIL 70

A CERTAIN PERCEPTION...74

A PERCEPTION OF BLACKNESS 82

LAW, JUSTICE & LIBERTY 88

GENESIS REVISITED 100

IS WOMAN WOMAN BY VIRTUE OF A CERTAIN DISABILITY? 119

CREATION: FROM GOD TO MAN...126

THE OMNICOSMIC RAMBLINGS 132

BEING AND BECOMING 138

A PAROXYSM OF BEWILDERMENT 142

BRYAN'S TRIBUTE...148

SECTION 361: CAPITULATION OR ENLIGHTENMENT.....................................154

CARNIVAL AND ITS EMBRACE OF NAKEDNESS............................159

CRIME AND THE FAMILY 166

EGREGIOUS IRRESPONSIBILITY (As I See It) 172

HAIR, HERE AND THERE..177

LUCIAN POLITICS AMONG THE DOCTORS 180

PAROLE 186

THE PIAYE SAGA 193

THE HUG THAT ROCKED THE WORLD.............................198

THE METAPHYSICS OF CORRUPTION.............................202

THE HOLE 205

THE NEW PARADIGM 210

THE QUINTESSENCE OF ASININITY 214

THE SACRIFICIAL LAMB...218

THE CREATION OF THE RUDY JOHN BEACH PARK: LABORIE 223

THE JOY OF DYING 235

APHORISMS

ALPHA 239

ARMAGEDDON..239

BEAUTY 240

BEING 241

BEING AND NOTHINGNESS 241

CAVEAT 241

CYNICISM 242

DECEMBER INTERLUDE 242

DEATH 242

EGO..243

EXAMS 243

FRIENDSHIP 243

HOMO SAPIENS 244

HELL 244

HUMILITY...244

INTEGRITY 245

INTENTION...245

JUSTICE 245

KNOWLEDGE 245

LAW 246

THE LAWYER 246

LA VIE 247

LAUGHTER (1) 247

LAUGHTER (2)...247

LIFE (1) 248

LIFE (2) 248

LIFE (3) 248

LOVE (1) 249

LOVE (2)..249

LOVE (3)..249

MANHOOD 250

OMEGA..250

POLITICS..251

REALITY 252

RELIGION 252

SHE... 252

TAKE TIME...253

THE BLACKMAN............................... 254

THE CAUSE..254

THE CIRCLE 255

THE FUTURE.................................... 255

THE IDEALIST (1) 256

THE IDEALIST (2) 256

THE MEDIA 257

THE SEARCH..257

THE SEXES 257

YOU 258

VICTORY..258

WISDOM 259

WOMAN 259

POEMS

LOVING PEACE 261

THE EXISTENTIAL PARADOX 262

FOR YOU 264

A DREAM 265

A DIME..266

THE CHALICE...267

COMMITTED 268

DYING 269

SHOULD I 270

A WINTER'S SUMMER 271

INDIGNATION 272

THE PEARL..273

THE DREAM 274

MADNESS 275

THE PARADOX...277

THE STRANGER..279

REFLECTIONS

LOVE[1]

The phenomenon of love has perplexed the minds of men on both definitional and operational levels. It is something you know all about when not asked; but when confronted with the question, "What is love?", you surprisingly but truly find your assumed knowledge reduced to "perhaps", "but", "you know"; and in the conflicting morass of your explanations you find yourself essentially reduced to a state of stuttering idiocy or enlightened ignorance. And all one really hears is the whispering of a heart in love.

Perhaps that is where the answer lies. Not in the heart but in that gentle whisper that pervades one's entire being, holds the sceptre of the heart and occupies the throne of the mind. It is that whisper of life that establishes the nexus between oneself and the universe. It constitutes that sole / "soul" reason for wanting to be with them. It is the life-blood, the elan vitae of your existence. It is the basis of your universal desire. What constitutes that whisper? Is it human? Is it rational? Is it seeing or is it blind, unknowing, atavistic? It is very human, but in the mystic process of revelation it transcends man's finitude and his madness. It is rational, or its existence lies in your perception of the unity of becoming in a being. It is a question of

---

[1] This reflection, and where relevant, applies to the Man and Woman in their singularity and plurality.

10

RAMBLINGS OF A MIND &
PULSATIONS OF A HEART

coming to grips with the universe in the unity of one person, her/ him. It is a question of addressing yourself to all the dimensions of your being and seeing reflected in the mirror of herself/ himself the path to the ultimate justification of yourself.

However he/she transcends this instrumentality, for she/ he not only is the path, she/he is also that which you seek. Though she/he is the end, yet paradoxically he/she is not; for the end would imply stagnation, sterility. And love is by no means sterile. It is the epitome of dynamic, sublime rationality. With her/him a process of spiritual growth begins. She/he is not love. You are not love. It is only in relationship that love is personified. You are an instrument of love; she/he is an instrument of love; and it is only in concert that the music of the spheres can be created. Though you are an instrument yet love is of yourself. You are its source and yet its agent. She/he is the end and yet the beginning. Such is the paradox of love. But it is a paradox that can be understood: for love is rational.

If love is rational, is it then devoid of emotion?
If love is rational, is it then cold and petrifying?
If love is rational, can it then be computerised?

The answer to each of these questions is a definitive No. Rationality and emotion coexist in us the lovers of the universe; each is a side of the coin of human perception and reality. Hence love is knowledge and an appreciation of that knowledge. However, it must be realised that since Man is a point of a continuum of evolving life so is his reality of love proportionately manifested in relation to that degree of evolution. It would be irrational for man to experience love on a level that was beyond him.

If love is knowledge how does one "fall" in love? One does not fall in love or into love. What then is the genesis or provenance of that perception and knowledge? How does the process really begin? A very interesting question, and here is my answer. But first, let us dispose with this question. Is the beginning superior to the end? On an essential level of abstraction the answer is a categorical No. To go a little further, the unity of love has no beginning and no end. When a love relationship ends it is not love that has ended, it is you that have strayed off the path of love or has foundered on a shoal in the ocean of love. A shoal of your own creation however manifest.

A LIKELY PROCESS OF GROWTH

When you first saw her/him you were attracted, perhaps: and then you met her/him and you talked. She/he was interesting and interested, and so were you. She/he was pleasant, and so your affectionate response mechanism not being warped, you liked her/him. You liked what you perceived and so in time you were laughing with her/him in the sunshine. It was a learning process. As she/he opened one dimension of herself/himself, your mind grasped its contents. It is logical for the mind to have an affinity for the beautiful, the orderly, and the sublime. The mind strives for that which is logical since the very quiddity of the mind and its intrinsic operational goal is logic. Hence the deranged mind, the warped mentality cannot be logical, cannot be beautiful in its contemplative mode on a regressive template.

Later, in the candour of her/his trust she/he being so very human gives you a glimpse of her/his inadequacies and limitations. You knew her/him. A universal link is revealed and perceived. Now you know her/him: her/his faults, limitations, inadequacies are at the portals of your judgement. Do you judge or do you in your magnificent humility accept? Is it the sum total of her/his being? What is the summation of yourself? Logical, rational questions.

Transcending your base origin, you realise that her/his virtues and possibilities constitute the scale of infinity. And you also realise that in communion with her/him, the parameters of her/his being would approximate this infinitude. At this point in the process you have in great measure, addressed yourself to the seeming totality of her/his being. You are now aware of the essential differences that exist between herself/himself and yourself, and on so many levels. You do not want to change her/him, nor make him/her an extension of yourself, your ego. You want her/him as perceived and known, though knowing that in loving tenderness, you both would change and be changing each other as you both progressed in the spiritual growth process of love. He/she is your Alpha and your Omega, and yet you both know that the curtain of the dawn has only just been raised.

At this point you have a partial fullness of knowledge and appreciation. The heart and mind are united. You have decided: she/he has decided. A promise is made: a judgement is passed unknowingly and acceptance crowns the heart of one's expectations and anticipations. Is that the end? Do you have a storybook ending to love forever and ever and be happy?

Love is a state of being in which you invest all, not part, of yourself; every moment of your existence. That is difficult and yet so beautiful. In your relationship of love there is need for tolerance, for understanding, for faith, and of course forgiveness.

Man is mortal and therefore weak. And so the fight in love for love must go on. It is indeed a struggle predicated upon this intrinsic weakness. A struggle from within with the external. But as one wins each trying day, the easier it becomes to maintain that state of being. Both she and you are the essential equations in this formula of love. You both have to act, to do, with and for each other. However there will be in your togetherness many lapses, for you both are human. There will be much to forgive; but there is hope: for man is spiritual in his possible fruits: and forgiveness is indeed a spiritual act. To forgive is indeed divine. To know, to give, to share, to understand, to be faithful, and to forgive – these are the cardinal virtues of love. Love could not exist or be experienced without this combination. Love is sublime and holistic communion with another.

To keep her/him you will have to be true to yourself: for it is only in being true to yourself that you can be true to the integrity of his/her person. You have heard so much about the youthful exuberance of the male: his natural quest or thirst for adventures. Look deeply and you will realise that her meadows and valleys are as verdant with every passing moment. Explore the countryside of your togetherness and you both will discover many a vale of flowers. Take time to look and you will discern her face blushing in the sunshine of your adoration. Take time my friend, for the field is never green on the other side or by the other side. It is a spurious hue for therein lies the beasts of your concupiscence, lasciviousness and greed. Do not think that the extent of your carnal peregrinations is in direct proportion to your manhood. The contrary is true. For as you play the field you are undermining your masculinity, warping your finer sensibilities and perpetuating a monstrous injustice on her and yourself.

It does not take long to be tainted by the unwholesomeness of your misdeeds, your exploits, and your nocturnal inequities. And as you regress in your infantile beastiality, the temper of your relationship with her unconsciously and even consciously deteriorates. You will in time have changed. For a man does change by the constancy of his actions, his misdeeds. And though this may sound farfetched, your physical appearance and outward demeanour will reflect the moral cancer you are contaminated with. Your moral bankruptcy will be evident and your perversions will have numbed your finest, salubrious moral and spiritual awareness. By then you will have strayed from the path of love - perhaps irrevocably.

Manhood has never been a consequence of a state attendant to one's chronological status, nor masculinity an index of a man's carnal exploits, which in many instances are mere vapid extensions of a febrile and degenerate imagination caught in a vortex of impotence. To be a Man or Woman, you have to be true to yourself as such. And being "true" means simply, not simplistically, being able to look at yourself in the mirror of your life and say: "I am proud of the being within the person I see". When you can say that in all sincerity, with all authenticity of self, then you are a Man or a Woman. The world will not shout it at you. Why? That would be superfluous since you already know who and what you are. To be masculine or feminine means the honourable expression of your sexual identity in a situation of social representation.

It takes a man or woman with a high sense of moral courage to walk the path of love. The walk however can be done but only in and with the dignity of your manhood or womanhood. The temptation to gaze and graze in the surrounding fields and valleys of passion is great. But then when you have embarked on the path of love, you are not alone. She is with you: you are with her. You both are the path and together you both shall find the grail of your universal. It is only in loving communion, which constitutes the sum and substance of human, that man can give unequivocal proof of his masculinity and manhood. She likewise.

In the realm of love there is no room for prostitution of self. And this prostitution can occur on a verbal, action and in-action level: sins of commission and omission. By his infidelity, oral, carnal or otherwise, the man can reduce his capacity to establish a mature and permanent relationship. He can undermine his emotional stability, become rationally myopic and live in a world of crass rationalisations. He ceases to be a man: and becomes a "noman" for the thing in the mirror is, to say the least, a miserable excuse of and for a man.

What would her reaction be if he became a "noman"?

THE PROCESS OF REGRESSION AND REBIRTH

In time she would become aware of a certain hiatus in the chain of their relationship. Her heart is troubled. The possibility of a final dissolution strikes her to the ground.

Her knees are like jello and she crawls in a pool of tears. There is pain, there is pathos, there is trauma, there is anguish: her heart is broken. But he does not see. In the silence of the night and in the emptiness of her world, she weeps like a child. She wants him and in her crisis she calls out his name. He cannot hear her, for the gurgling sound of beer and the brazen laughter of another drowns out her cries. She reaches out for him but to no avail. She cannot reach him, for unknown to them both, he is already beneath and beyond her. Therein lies the tragedy. In the twilight of the day she falls asleep and in the dark she turns in unto herself and as the cocoon of sleep envelops her, she metamorphoses into something less sensitive, more durable, more resilient and more resourceful. She has attained a novel form of independence.

The dawn breaks. The sunshine is invigorating but she does not smile. She has lost the capacity for laughter.

He arrives.

HIS CRISIS

The doormat of his affection is no longer there. In her place he perceives a stranger. A stranger that is indeed alien because her present responses are novel and unprepared for. He is aware of the emptiness in her eyes: a certain disturbing vacuity and aloofness in her demeanour. His knees buckle and as he strikes the pavement of his awareness, it hits him: He has lost her.

To lose another especially if one is at fault, if one never intended the loss is a heart rendering, mind shocking experience. The world which he at one point helped to create and the pillars of which he has now undermined crashes at his feet. His once dormant love now rushes madly through the veins of his being. He needs her and he wants her. He knows now that life has no meaning without her. Now at last, all others pale in significance and only she can save him morally, emotionally, rationally and existentially. In desperation he implores, importunes, exhorts and pleads. But she is adamant. She has decided, made a promise and passed a judgement. She asks him to accept the bald fact of their separation. The door closes.

DOES SHE LOVE HIM?

The roots of love are quite durable. That is his consolation coupled with the resolve to mend himself, his ways, and to find her. He knows now that in the fires of his crisis the moral fibres of his being have been transmuted into something far superior to what they were. Man has indeed the capacity to change: he always had. He must now find her since it is now pellucid to him that she is the main-spring of his life and that intuitively, he knows that she loves him even though she might at this time be blind to this hope generating fact. The spark as he sees it is there: how can he fan it aflame?

He knows that he must be around and about her, and yet at the same time he must project an intention of coolness. It would be fool hardy to take a direct approach; he would only be treading on the corns of her resentment and seeming disaffection. But how can he be cool when he is overwhelmed by his love for her. Yet he must. But for how long? The torture, the pain, the ambivalence created by his mind and heart are excruciating. To win he must be by her side and yet not overwhelm her. She now has her full independence and can flaunt it in his face. The thought staggers him. How does she spend her evenings? That was almost a fatal shot. He must stop thinking or he will go insane. He can hardly stand the stress, the strain. Yet he must be cool. It is madness. Can he think of the future? No. The day is enough to overcome him yet his being saved lies in the hope, the promise of the future.

Despite the intense pain he stays around and pretends that he does not see, he does not care: it hurts. He helps her now and then without telling her that he is willing to help her all his life. He walks and talks with her without hinting that he could walk the longest mile despite his aching corns. He is around and about her but yet be Mr. Joe Cool. Everything he does for her he knows that he could it to the nth degree. He loves her: but does she really know it? She dances with another: he does not cry. He is a man. He bleeds instead. Should he join them at the dance and then cut in? At present that would be too much. He must be Mr. Joe Cool. In the pool of his anguish she has taught him to swim and after he had learnt, she places him in the heat of the desert where no oasis of hope seemed to exist. And now he was being roasted by the passion of his affection and tortured by millions of grains of blowing sand – elements of his dreams and memories. Yet he must be Mr. Joe Cool.

The days pass by reluctantly with him shuffling his feet in the sands of time. The emptiness is smothering and the pain in his eyes could be discerned by any lover. He is around and about her but not overshadowing her. Always helpful, always waiting patiently, very patiently. The indomitable faith that the love she bore for him is still there, keeps him going. He is Sysiphus and carrying his rock on his shoulders in questioning futility. He has perused the works of the Stoics and concluded that they have never been in love. He challenges the works of Plato and discovers that his world of ideas and platonic love was lost in the caves of Greece. His salvation does not lie in philosophy. His salvation lies in something tangible, something warm, something gentle and something human - her. The pain is increasing and he increases the pain as he claws his heart with his mind. But he is around and about her: the forever Mr. Joe Cool.

The hawk of time flew many a mile of days before she displayed a whisper of concern. He was around and about her when it happened. By now she had seen him many a time and despite herself was aware of his simulated gaiety. With the eyes of her love she glimpsed the carnage within, and her heart reacted with the anguish at that sight. He played and he laughed and she marvelled at his coolness, at the mastery over himself. She did not know what he knew so painfully that he was her slave. Her arctic attitude began disintegrating very rapidly. Now she had where she had always wanted. He knew her and she knew him in their nakedness, and she longed for his love, his strength his masculinity. They had shared so once upon a time: should all those moments of tenderness, all those dreams and intentions be wasted on the desert air? He was still in the desert.

They had known each other for a very long time. Could not that time be bridged by the present to the future? Her heart was in turmoil. He came to her and saw tears in her eyes. His heart quickened. Very calmly he wiped the tears from her eyes. They did not know that it was a symbol of peace and reconciliation - a surrendering of defences.

Lying on her back she thought of him; and he lying on his back he thought of her. The personality of Mr. Joe Cool had become very oppressive. He felt that he should take a stand: for a man must take a stand sometime. He got up and stood by the phone. The persona of Joe Cool was now a thing of the past. With this new freedom he exercised purposefully his fingers on the dial. There was a gentle lull: she answered. It was good. They were again on the path of love.

As Gibran wrote in the Prophet, *"if love finds you worthy it shall direct your path"*. The key word in this statement is "worthy". And it is worthiness that gives love its moral base. For love is the unselfish giving of one's self to another. Should one give of one's self if one is not worthy of one's self? And going a bit further should one give of one's self to another if that self is not worthy of that other? Hence in love there must be a moral compatibility which is given expression in the reciprocality of knowledge, understanding, fidelity and trust. To love is the greatest responsibility that a man or woman can undertake; and it is one to which they both should address themselves to quite seriously. Is it fair and just to play with the life of another, her hopes and her dreams?

Is it fair and just to explore her fascinating possibilities under the guise of a spurious relationship? Is it fair, is it just to accept the pledge of another when one's person is divided among so many? These are the questions that a man must ask when he finds himself in the situation of love: where the party is prepared and willing to sacrifice her person on the altar of a manifest concern which is essentially contrived. Love is beautiful, so very beautiful and yet there are so many who because of it are languishing in despair and despondency Should it always be a Mr. Joe Cool? No one can use love as a plaything with impunity. Love is not singleness: it is wholeness and wholesomeness. It is sublime salubriousness. It is never one but two who are involved in this joyful communion.

When you find her, hold on to her for she in the final analysis is your "soul" reason for being. The man who loses the contest of love has lost himself and his life.

Can one and be loved without discipline? The answer is a categorical No. For discipline is orderliness: it implies direction and purpose. Love is not chaotic: it is not the mere assemblage of affects. As has been stated earlier, it is a state of being. On this very human level it is "becoming" and yet at the same time "it is". The former reflects the dynamism of love, the latter its infiniteness. The dynamism implies involvement and this involvement is another term for doing. Since love encompasses the entire self one must of voluntary necessity work at the operational aspects of love. There is need for consistency which calls for a type of determination, a type of discipline. For though love is of is of the infinite, he man is finite with feet of clay. He cannot escape his rather mundane, terrestrial environment: he cannot be oblivious to distracting elements and insalubrious propensities. He has to fight himself for love with love.

For it is only when he has conquered himself that he can be himself totally and love totally.

The fight must and can only be a rational, conscious determination on his part to be faithful to her, to his commitments and to himself. Its moral worth lies in the fact that it is conscious and rational and that is based on the supreme principle that love is the total giving of oneself to another, not in the context of servitude or blind adoration but with the knowledge that the voluntary giving of self is a prerequisite to life and love is life. Life is not darkness: it is not nihilism. Life is order, symmetry, harmony, plenitude and enlightenment. Love is all of those things and more. It is discipline and yet it is freedom; it is beauty and it is truth. It is not license, it is not servitude. It is the giving and the taking in sublime reciprocity on a level that nullifies the giving and the taking: two separate beings are no longer separate but are fused or united in a very loving communion. And yet under this rubric of ineffable togetherness man and woman stand in their singular splendour and purposefulness.

Though it is true that there is need of conscious involvement in the situation of love, yet it is not meant that one has to be perpetually reminding oneself that one's behaviour, one's attitude should reflect that involvement. Once the pattern of love has been set it transcends the mechanical level of conscious reminding; it becomes a way of life and the very degree of involvement infuses every action, every word with its sublime, celestial, creative beneficence. It does not need constant articulation since "it is"; and it is the question of "being" that makes of your love, the unreflected love. It pervades your entire existential field and makes of your terrestrial sojourn the ideal prelude to eternity.

"There is beggary in the love that can be reckoned," (Shakespeare). Love is infinite and by virtue of this quality it implies the existence of other dimensions of being. It is extra cosmic and therefore rises above the boundaries of our rather finite situation. It encompasses man and woman, their world and their life and raises them to a level that is yet very human but spiritual. To be God-like, man must first be aware of and realise the potentialities of being human. And this can only be achieved with and through the instrumentality of love. Love has no boundaries, no limitations; it transcends all pseudo constraints of ethnicity, race, creed and nationality. It is man qua man and woman qua woman that are involved. All other qualifications become grossly insignificant and should be relegated to limbos of obscurity. No one race, no one people has a monopoly on love; for love is catholic. It is above man's parochialism, is myopism, his bigotry and madness.

It is indeed true that the human subject has no intrinsic aversion to establishing profound, meaningful relationships with another of its kind, irrespective of race, colour or ethnicity. Any revulsion manifested must be attributed to cultural conditioning: a reflection of the warped and distorted perspective of a social system and its system members. Love is not specific: it sees no colour for it is colourful. And to say that love must restrict itself in terms of colours and ethnic specificity is to admit to one ethical infantilism and guttural and atavistic propensities: a bathos of absurdity: a philosophy of the pavement. In the world of love there is no room for hypocrisy, for bigotry. There cannot be. For love removes the veil of primeval conceit that enshrouds us and clads us in a cloak of a universal humanism.

There is a bond that unites all loves of the world, and this bond which is a reflection of the commitment to a life of fidelity, trust and understanding is also a symbol of their participation, their supreme and salutary involvement in the life of another. The bond is also an expression of their universal desire. There is no imperative that the lovers of the world must unite; that would be nonsensical since the lovers of the world are specifically and generally united. It is of vital importance that you become aware of the catholicity of love and not allow your life and hers to be defined in terms of a stultifying outlook, very archaic, anachronistic and which places as it were blinders on your vision of the phenomenon of love.

Love is not to be restricted: it is not to be cramped, confined, strait-jacketed. It loves the wide and open spaces; and in your heart and hers there are indeed meadows of beauty, simplicity, truth and openness. Let your love and hers flourish on the plains of your understanding and togetherness: and which in essence is a disciplined acceptance of her fragilities and yours: and including also her uniqueness and your differences.

INFATUATION[2]

In dealing with this topic we do not think it possible to give a concise and unequivocal definition of of the term Infatuation, nor do we think it essential as far as the general intention and context of our writing is concerned. We shall endeavour to use a certain method and by so doing make some observations and throw some light on this perplexing relational situation.

Unlike love, infatuation is essentially ephemeral. Whereas love addresses itself to the totality of the person within the circumstance of a sublime, authentic relationship, infatuation on the other hand manifests itself on a more superficially, physical and sensually oriented level. The two are quintessentially poles apart though they are so often mistaken and spuriously equated. With infatuation there is a crass acquisition, a wanting to possess: not for mutual enjoyment and which would be incidental to the process, but for self, ego satisfaction. A compound element of lasciviousness prevails and all one hears is the maddened flow of passion rushing through the veins of ones concupiscence and cupidity. One sees, and one is arrested by what seems to be a vision of feminine pulchritude. The senses reel, the knees tremble like jello and the nerves become taut

---

[2] Singularity and plurality in relation to the genders can be exchanged if considered relevant.

like guitar strings. It must be realised that all this take place on an essentially perceptual and physical level.

The initial and subsequent movement is influenced primarily by the physical attributes of the female. The male by virtue of his primordial animalism is impelled to action; but then being man, and that is an organism that possesses a rational faculty regardless how limited, and tempered by an aesthetic-ethical flavour, acquired advertently or inadvertently by virtue of his societal peregrinations, he endeavours consciously or subconsciously to rationalise the simian attraction or affect. It is a rationalism that seems tantamount to sublimation: but is not. So that now man through his purple vision perceives himself as being a victim of the inexorable process of man's biological, affectional destiny. "Male and female" he created them a companion one for the other, till the planet becomes a very visible, squashing, crunching, squeezing manifestation of their explosive fecundity.

Infatuation is temporary: it is evanescent. By its very immediacy creates delusions of perennially. It is an obsession on the level of the physical; and as such it can blind ones inner vision, colour ones judgement and reduce homo sapiens to the level of his primordial biological imperative. The object of infatuation, that is the female, is not seen in the integrity of her person, her very human attributes and potentialities. She is just an adjunct to the male's immediate and conjured needs and desires. She is a veritable extension of his ego and a victim of his id; and the tragic element in this pathetic drama is that both parties are essentially ignorant of the other's real posture in this scheme of things.

You the male proclaim your concern and manifest a certain adoration and even helplessness. You have fallen in love the bard writes. And sure enough it is a fall. Just as in war you have fallen, so "in love" you have fallen: victims instead of victors. For one instant your desires are self initiated and self oriented. There is no universal communion and of course no authenticity. On a cushion of hot air, the heat of your passion, you seem to float not realising that you are moving towards an encounter of sordid consummation with another. You have arrived at the mythical city of Eldorado: the city of gold.But of the myth you do not know: she does not know until it is too late.

Infatuation—puppy love: that of course reflects one's sexual maturational development or should we say misdevelopment. Emotional cretism might be a better description of the event and what it entails. Is one's present situation one of infatuation or one of love? What really is the test? Is your seeming perceptiveness and confidence the index of emotional maturity? Perhaps if she professes to be unhappy within the embrace of your encounter, are you prepared to set her free with loving understanding and sensitivity? Sometimes the most loving act is to allow another to go his or her own way. Infatuation is a cage. Love is freedom. In the former, you may and can imprison yourself and another. In the latter, the sky is your background, and the universe your playing field. Others shall join you there and the music of the heart and of the spheres shall provide the melody to the beat of your life and hers.

FEMALE DIGNITY

I t has been said that a woman is a woman by virtue of a certain incapacity or disability; this, of course, is indeed a gross articulation of supreme idiocy. Its implication is that there is a certain fundamental imbalance between her and her counterpart, man: an imbalance which is female and negatively oriented. Woman is woman, and man is man, and by virtue of their unique differences, they complement each other in living situations of equality. She is your equal, and you are her equal, and the bond that exists between her and yourself is an expression of that equality.

In the fullness of her femininity, there is dignity, and it is her consciousness of that dignity that makes it possible for her to accept you in the plenitude of your masculinity, and in the complex totality of your differences and sameness. Your relationship with her should not be one of dominion and submission. She is a human being just like yourself and, as such, is fundamentally a free agent, who, in conscious volition, has embarked upon a relationship that sublimates her individual independence, innate freedom, and intrinsic situational equality. The bond of love is not a badge of servitude. She does not love in order to become a slave. She does not surrender her person in order to become your footstool. In love, there is no surrendering, for to surrender would imply a situation of conquest.

In love, there is only a giving and a taking which is nullified by an overwhelming reciprocity, so that the two elements are fused in communion.

The question of male chauvinism has no place in a male relationship. Love is authentic and wholesome and should not be instrumental in meeting the inadequacies of one's ego at her expense. To proclaim your superiority is to expose your inferiority, your unsureness of yourself. A spurious ego lift will not heal the faults in your personality. It will be foolhardy on your part to endeavour to overwhelm her with your maleness: she would only rebel or cower in submission. The first response would lead to a state of conflict which would be diametrically opposed to a state of love. The latter expression would result in a situation that would be pregnant with seeds of hate. She would despise you as a man and her very silence would be an indictment of your gross failure.

If you are a man, if you know who and what you are, there is no need to proclaim your manhood. But if you are not what you proclaim to be, then the fault lies not with her but with you. Her seeming threat to you will only be a reflection of your smallness. You will want to dominate, to subdue, for the very simple and patent reason that in her female dignity and strength, she will be a mirror to your person: and the face in the mirror will either be that of a slave or a rat. At this point in your relationship which is at best just a morbid symbiosis, you will have stepped off the path of love: for love as has been previously defined, if it finds you worthy, will direct your course. Your worthiness will be abundantly clear, and in your blindness - and chauvinism is a blinding affliction – you will have regressed to the level of a sophisticated human animal. Love, truth, and beauty will have eluded you, and like a king of the dark, you will be grovelling in the dirt of your passions searching for worms of pleasure. She will have left you: with dignity.

VIRGINITY

From the onset, we think it of cardinal significance to address ourselves to what is or is not virginity: or who is or is not a "virgin" and the implications thereof. According to customary parlance, a "virgin" is one who has never assumed a horizontal or other posture, while in-depth penetration of her genitals is being effectuated by the complementary organ of the male. It is indeed lamentable that on the basis of this rather superficial definition, regardless of how invasive, that so many do make value judgments as far as the worth and value of the human individual are concerned.

How anyone with any modicum of integrity and maturity could use a purely physical yardstick to measure a being that transcends the physical? Holding on to the above definition, one hears value judgments of this nature: "I will never marry a "non-virgin". The facility with which all "knowing" and all "experienced" males make an issue with and of a tissue is indeed incredible; and the reasons which are given to justify their position, in truth and in fact, amount to a rationalisation of their own inadequacy and their patent and gross inability to view the vast and complex panorama of human sexuality and place it in its correct perspective. This attitude is symptomatic of psycho-socio maturational uncertainties, and that the attendant rationalisation is bastardised reasoning and a prostitution of reality.

If at the stage of your development you have to hold on to this pedestrian concept of "virginity" and the attendant judgmental attitude of the pavement, then we do categorically state that "virginity" should be perceived as atavistic, Neanderthal. We have in our time met **"virgins"** who were pleasant, charming, quite prepossessing, whose integrity was beyond question, and whose probity of conduct was indeed laudable. But then on the other hand, we have also met **"virgins"** who in no uncertain terms were merely sophisticated human animals, uncouth and unprincipled. From this it can be seen that virginity as is now commonly comprehended is no valid criterion for making a value judgement as far as our womenfolk are concerned.

(To the girls): Since we tend to associate virginity with virtuousness we pose these questions. Are you a virgin and therefore virtuous, if you sequester yourself in your room – alone of course – and spend your fettered fury in a bed of useless desire? Are you less virtuous because within the context of a meaningful relationship your lover has explored your fascinating possibilities? Are you a virgin, are you virtuous if you embark on a course of lascivious excursions or exercises, but calculatingly preclude the possibility or actuality of penile penetration? These are indeed interesting questions. But the fundamental issue is, what are you, and which is intimately related to who you are. If you ladies are asked by some misguided and presumptuous male as to what you are, your answer most unequivocally should be this:

"I am what I am: and by virtue of what I am I can add to the splendour and gaiety of life, to the sum of human achievements and to the aspirations of human ecstasy. In short I am a woman, a woman in the ideal sense of the word, and perhaps and within the bosom of time I can get to know another in the sublime and salubrious mystery of our passion."

What really is the significance of her being *"virgo intacta"*, when she, the subject and love of your love and affection, is fundamentally the sum total of her experiences? Bereft of this or that experience, what is it you are left with? Certainly not the individual before you. And so an experiential castration or lobotomy would leave you poorer and reveal in its putrid nudity, your obscene egoism and maturational myopia.

Each and every one of you has his shoe of expectation and like the prince with the glass slipper, you traverse the course of your life hoping to find the elegant, the delicate foot that fits. But then this, which for the most part is forged in a furnace of idealism, must of necessity be tempered with an element of realism and human understanding. To embark on a quest for a goddess is to expose your egotistical vanity and gross, crass overestimation of yourself.

Your exercise in this respect will be nugatory: only delusions and profound disappointment will await you at the end of your quixotic quest. But if in your cognisance of human frailties and weaknesses you can perceive beauty, loveliness, greatness of character, truth, and fidelity in another, then you are worthy of love and of being loved. Relegate the ghosts of her past to a grave of obscurity and hold on to the present in all its glorious plenitude, and the loving tenacity of your grasp will transmute the future, and together, and for all time, you two shall share the grail of your universal desire.

Why be overwhelmed and find it incomprehensible by the fact that she has "made love" with another at a time and in the past when your existence was of no consequence: when for all intent and purposes you were not even born? Should she by some mystical revelation have anticipated your coming, your arrival upon the scene of her life? **(Ridiculous.)** Did you anticipate her coming and thus held yourself in solemn readiness? The answer in the vast majority would be No. But if your answer to this question was in the affirmative, what really would be the situation, and what really are its implications? Of course, it would be the sexual. It is the sexual that is being controlled, constrained, directed, regimented. But then the sexual is one of the many dimensions of the totality of one's person. Does the constraint placed upon one's sexual proclivity make one a whole person?

Does it endow one with the attributes of warmth, gentleness, understanding, and maturity? Does it of necessity enhance one's humanity and of course one perception and perspicacity? The answer, of course, is no. What about one's deportment, probity of conduct, degree, and manner of relating with others, and above all, one's spirituality? And in this regard, we are alluding to one's eschatological posture in terms of the moving and goal-oriented stream of humanity.

Our contention is that one can be a "virgin" and still be a miserable excuse for a man or woman. Is it merely her continence that makes her worthy of you or you of her? If that is the case, you both are then to be pitied, and in your blindness and smallness, you both deserve each other. If your view is in consonance with ours, hold on to her in the immediacy of your situation. If you fail to hold, and that could be a pattern of your life, you may find yourself in a situation of confused despair, writing something akin to this:

I perhaps know what I am looking for;
I perhaps have seen what I am looking for;
But I have not found what I am looking for.
The course of my life has been and is
A rather tortuous one;
And perhaps I will have lost
When I have found
What I am looking for.

It has been said that man, as opposed to woman, is polygamous by nature and that it is the mores of his society that have coerced him into surrendering this innate privilege of his maleness. And so the questions, to which we shall address ourselves, are:

1. Is man intrinsically polygamous?
2. If so, is the mores of his monogamous society an affront to his intrinsic being?
3. Is polygamy and the further evolution of mankind compatible?

With regard to the first question, what is being asked is this: has man, just by being male, a certain proclivity or an innate propensity to having many or several mates? The history of man has evidenced this phenomenon. In other words, the evidence that has been culled from the present and past civilisations preponderates in favour of the male in this respect: that is, as regards that type of acquisitive behaviour. When the two genders are considered, it would seem that that type of behaviour pattern does not really amount to an aberration in the seemingly natural scheme of human conduct.

In the society of the cave, the extent of one's acquisition was a function of brute strength and sometimes cunning. Even on the animal level, this state of affairs is evidenced. And by possessing, the acquisitive instinct was being expressed. To what extent this instinct was given expression was dependent on the acquisitor's strength. And in terms of man, where life was lived on a rather rudimentary level, the superiority of his brutish strength was made abundantly clear. He possessed: and of the possessor, he expected a certain dumb allegiance which reflected his claim of ownership.

Even today in our rather sophisticated society, this allegiance or quasi-allegiance is expected of the female possessor by the male. The feminist movement has in no way altered this situation. On the contrary, it has made the hiatus that exists between the genders in terms of that specific pattern of conduct more pronounced. The feminists cry out or flaunt their "independence," but in so doing, they do not give expression to that acquisitive instinct. They maintain that they are free to establish associations with as many males as possible, and they do. They are free spirits. But do they like their male counterparts regard their consorts or lovers as their possession? Do they really and instinctively expect a certain allegiance from their male "associates"? The answer is No. And that is an essential difference. However, they do try to seek a convenient and functional equality. It would seem that throughout the ages, this acquisitive instinct of the male became more expressive, but up to a point; whereas that of the female became limited or even stunted because of her intrinsic biology and her sub and consequent social posture that was a product of her biological genesis.

Another point that should be noted is that when at the dawn of history, man stood before the entrance of his cave and faced the unknown, where was his female possessor? Besides him, in front of him, behind him, or within the cave? We hold that she was behind and within the cave, suckling and protecting her young. The man, the male, was the great protector, protecting woman because she was the bearer of his seed, the mother of his offspring, the satisfier of his needs on whatever level. She was his prized possession. With his brutish strength and emerging cunning, he endeavoured to meet the exigencies of his primitive world and existence. And if in a bloody confrontation with the elements of the unknown, he was coerced into surrendering his mortality, then another male took his place as the great protector. We are of the opinion that the mortality rate at that time was indeed much higher among the males as compared to the females. Why didn't the female claim the right to have and own several mates in light of those harsh statistics? Is it that being female and maternal dulls the edge of her acquisitiveness in terms of the male, because of the demands placed upon her by her childbearing possibilities and responsibilities and what they entail? Or is it that that instinct is a natural expression of a certain superiority on the level of brutish strength and primordial cunning? On the brute level, there seems to be an equation: gender superiority, physical superiority; and this is translated into acquisitiveness that is patently evidenced between genders. Also, it must be noted that the female childbearing role and function necessitated a certain dependence on the male.

As humankind evolved, as it relegated its brutish past, it can be said that the element of brute force has been sublimated into something essentially cerebral and human. From the lines of thought preceding this, it would seem that one is being drawn to the ineluctable conclusion that the male of the species is superior to the female. That is not so. The two, man and woman, are the essential and constitutive elements in the evolution of humankind. Without woman, man would never have evolved to the level of a human entity, and so the reality of humankind would be an abstraction reposing in the recesses of some cosmic mind.

Could the world as we know it, that is, in light of our present evolutionary status, continue to exist if it were devoid of the female presence? Assuming that as a result of some global cataclysm to which only woman was susceptible, and in consequence thereof, all of the women of the world in 2030 were to effect their terrestrial demise, and assuming further that at that point in time man had perfected the technological competence to manufacture only men in test tubes, since they had an unlimited supply of sperm and ova cells, what really would be the situation of "mankind" and humankind five hundred years hence? Here is man with all his brutish strength, his cerebral agility, and his seemingly only deprivation of woman's sexo-biological outlet. Is this the only function that the stream of "mankind" would be deprived of, and that is on a very essential level? A level that addresses itself to the very quiddity of man qua man. If this is the only deprivation, then by implication it is being admitted that the expression of her fecundity and sexuality constitutes the raison d'être of womankind. And that is not far from saying that she is on a purely functional and mechanistic level, the only level, the seminal spittoon of the universe.

With all the vehemence of our being, we declare that that cannot be. Her ontology, teleology, and eschatology are intimately entwined with that of man's, and they fit and complement each other in terms of the cosmological plan of the Godhead. Man and woman, he created them, whether by special creation or through the evolutionary process: the two constitute the coin of humanity. They are not alike, they are different, but they complement each other; and without the one, be it male or female, the coin of humanity would cease to be. And so the logical, rational conclusion that one can arrive at is that man without woman would regress: man without woman would cease to be: man without woman would be an impossibility. Each without the other would be a cosmological absurdity, a divine impossibility, since man and woman constitute the two sides of the face of God.

Returning to the issue of man's polygamous nature, which incidentally has led us down an interesting path of inquiry, it would seem that man's polygamous propensity is indeed a function of man's innate acquisitiveness in the society of the cave where the refinements of particularly human attributes were yet to manifest themselves at this juncture of human evolution. How far is the man of the present away from the door, the situation of the cave? A hundred thousand years at most, and that is like a grain of sand on one of the many beautiful beaches of the island of Saint Lucia: or a whisper of an event in the consciousness of the universe. And modern man is still polygamously inclined, but it is an inclination that is being transmuted, sublimated in terms of a more profound and self-fulfilling appreciation of the quintessential of his female counterpart –woman.

We shall at this juncture address ourselves to the second question, which is: "Are the mores of his monogamous society an affront to his intrinsic being"?

The answer to this question can very simply be answered monosyllabically: that is, no. But then there would be a subsidiary or supplemental question, and which is why. As has been made abundantly clear, the polygamous propensity of the male is characteristic of a being caught in the throes of a rather primitive existence. His finer sensibilities were yet to manifest themselves, as at this time his finest sensibilities have yet to be universally evidenced. At that point in the evolutionary process of humankind, man's brutish nature was in the ascendancy; the animal component was indeed quite evident, and so his rudimentary value system was a reflection of the prosaic and urgent exigencies of his existence. His perception of his normative system was not in terms of that crucial fundamental notion or construct of what "ought" to be, but in terms of the very concrete immediacy of his relational situation. The posture he assumed was not predicated on the finer virtues, the sanctity of human life, the dignity of the human person, and emanating therefrom the respect for her person, which are the features or attributes of our present civilisation. (We hope).

Thus, in the society of the cave, the imposition of a monogamous way of life would have been problematic, even an affront to the cave dweller. But man did not remain at the door of his cave. He traversed space and time in his sometimes blind quest for the ultimate fulfilment and justification of himself, and which could only be achieved in the shadow of his Creator. He is "being" and "becoming", and so the very quiddity of man is in a state of evolutionary flux. And yet when viewed through the perspective of his teleology and eschatology, one can discern a certain divine constancy.

And so as man takes more and more into his hands, the reins of his own evolution, he sublimates what may be regarded as the incidents of his very primitive past and in consequence thereof, that rational plurality that characterised his perception and actuality of his association with the other gender is being relegated to obscurity. This of course is an ongoing process: and hence vestiges of that proclivity are still evident. But the significant thing is that the male is viewing the female not only as the bearer of his seed, the mother of his children, but as a companion. And that presupposes a salubrious and functional equality in the dualism of mankind. He is aware that a plurality in terms of essential associations would be a prostitution of that indispensable dualism: would be demeaning of a woman's basic dignity and would be a slap at the two sides of the face of God. And so the emergence of a monogamous society is not an anomaly, a relational aberration, but a vital aspect of the evolutionary process of humankind.

Now this line of thought has taken us almost naturally into the third and last question. "Is polygamy and the further evolution of mankind compatible?" The evolutionary thrust is now maintained, sustained and directed by man and woman in conscious and subconscious volition. And it is a process that has as its *raison d'etre* the ultimate fulfilment of the subject on a level that transcends his/her temporal existence.

It is a process that raises on high those attributes of a budding humanity, fostered through thousands of years of upward groping, and which has made man and woman cognisant of their identical and eternal destiny. It must be noted that the very existence of man/woman is the extension and reification of divine love. And it is the principle of love translated in terms of the human situation that provides the necessary impulse in the streaming movements of human evolution.

Love is the essential catalyst in the actualisation of human potentiality. It is the Alpha and Omega in the whole human phenomenon, and it is the core value that validates the very existence of man and woman. She is a product of it. He is a product of it. And the two on an equal footing and in loving togetherness constitute the sum and substance of human life. Polygamy with its implied inequality of the two genders would be grossly obscene and incompatible with the further evolution of mankind, since it is an expression of a certain atavistic feature in the early genesis of the species.

As one becomes more and more involved in the unfolding process of one's relationship, the question of embarking on the ship of marriage becomes more and more urgent. Should one remain on shore secure in the status quo, or should one embark on a ship of one's creation that may at some uncertain time flounder on the reefs, the shoals of as yet unknown circumstance? A traumatic occurrence of inestimable magnitude.

To do or not to do: that really is the question. And as one's mind focuses on what seems so pleasantly imminent and on a rather abstruse level dreadful, one finds oneself in what essentially boils down to a crisis of freedom. The unfolding process continues on in its ineffable procession towards that certain point of the "alpha". To all third parties, the entire movement seems gradual, natural, and inexorable. But this is not so: for when one stands on the brink of one's bachelorhood, there is a pause. It is as though one's life and hers are noted, weighed, registered, and then fully accepted. And it is this acceptance with its very positive futuristic elements that provides the vital impulse, the will, to embark.

She has chosen: he has chosen. The choice has been made. What really should be the basis of that choice as far as her person and prospective companionship are concerned? This is indeed a very personal question which goes to the genesis, the continuity, and culmination of one's relationship. If through your heart and mind you can perceive the beauty and loveliness of character, of spirit, of personality: if you can perceive the gentleness of disposition and that gaiety of self and of life: if you can perceive all of these qualities and imbibe from this fountain of beauty, hold on to what you have been so fortunate to know and to experience. It is not the doing of big and momentous things that these qualities will disclose themselves. It will be in the doing of little things that you both do in common.

If the sunshine of her laughter, her gentle and pleasant casualness, and even justified annoyance can elicit within you a sense of contentment, understanding, and a feeling of reality, hold on. If she can temper your anger with her humour and tolerance and make you laugh even in spite of yourself, then you have a certain richness within your grasp, hold on. If she can colour your life's situation with her humility and glow unobtrusively in the irksome shadow of your quasi-companions, then you have authenticity within your orbit, hold on. If after a rather trying day you both can look at each other and conclude that life is indeed worth living, that there is joy and happiness to be had and to be shared, then hold on. Hold on to each other, and the choice will have been made, and the die will have been cast.

And in your serene security, you may sing her a song for you will be her greatest singer, or you may write her a poem for you will be her greatest poet. Perhaps you may even find yourself writing something akin to this:

Upon the shores of time, you stand
Immaculate in your nakedness
And like a pearl
Beneath a thousand waves of sea
You command all things
Within your sphere of radiance
Though delicately created
You reflect in your person
A Samson strength
Of beauty, loveliness, and grace
You are a pearl
Amidst a million grains of mortals
Who, in majestic simplicity,
And with the laughter of the sun,
Has enveloped me
In the regal folds of your person
~ *The Pearl*

However, in all of this, it has to be pellucidly understood that one has to be very realistic. In this situation, one is inclined to romanticise and to place another on a pedestal. Such indeed would be foolhardy; for regardless of the posture one may have assumed in terms of the other, one must never underestimate what a woman can and cannot do, will and will not do; and the commonality of the yardstick to be used is that patently indicated by the general experience of mankind. Never allow one's actual observational experience to be lulled into acceptance by one's expectations and over-estimations: for the soothing music of one's expectations can be the jingle of a meretricious melody.

When addressing oneself to the quiddity of marriage, one of necessity, must focus one's attention on one key term, **commitment**. It forms the greatest part of the marriage edifice; and if a structural fault emanates therefrom, then the marriage is like a sandcastle on one of the beaches of Terra del Fugeo. Its demise is only a matter of time, but certain. Within the marital realm, one is committed wholly and totally. A partial commitment will not suffice since it is tantamount to no commitment.

It is a giving of your whole in terms of the continued welfare of your "wholes". It is your life and her life that are crucially juxtaposed: and in this situation of aspirations, expectation, and trust, there is no room for games. It is a question of forsaking all others for the maintenance of the integrity of your togetherness. You are committed or should be committed to your marital life; and the constitutive elements of that life are primarily yourself and herself. All else is subordinate and should be instrumental in terms of one terminal value, the rectitude of your marriage. The term commitment connotes "being" and "becoming", and as such, continuous perpetual striving is implied. And that very continuity necessitates a functional discipline. In short, marriage is made a way of life, a way of being, perceiving, and doing: a *modus operandi* and a *modus vivendi*. And so within the universe of the term commitment, we have a conjunction of two fundamental elements: philosophy and morality.

There is another cardinal component in the structure of marriage, and that is fairness: fairness in terms of herself and yourself: fairness in terms of her doings and yours, fairness in terms of your expectations of her. The question of a double standard, whether in regard to matters of morality or mundane domesticity, has no part in a marital relationship. The probity of your conduct should in no way be on a lower and acceptable level simply because you happen to be a man, male, and masculine. It is sheer folly and blinding conceit to believe that she will be satisfied with this. There may be a seeming satisfaction which really is an acquiescence, giving rise to a growing resentment and distrust. Any double standard places undue strain in any relationship; and within the marriage context, such a posture assumed by either party is indeed inimical to the further and continued harmony of the whole. The question that one should always ask oneself is this: "if she were the one involved in my present affair or activity, would I be happy by my knowledge of it?". If the answer to that question is in the negative, then of necessity and of principle, one should immediately desist from that affair or activity. A corollary to the above is this: if she knew, would my present conduct be a source of joy and happiness to her? If one can address oneself objectively and with maturity to these two questions, then the significance of being fair becomes abundantly clear. And where this climate of fairness exists, one will find that life becomes easier to live; relationships blossom in the sunlight of a mutual trust, and problems and domestic discord are seen as areas for cooperation and for compromise. Marital life is not one big honeymoon: it is a journey towards a state of togetherness, of tranquility, and on that path, there are many sharp, pointed stones and pebbles: and it will be left to you both, by your determination, fortitude, trust, fidelity, and love, to blunt the teeth of adversity.

Within the sphere of the marital domestic situation, life is not one of continuous pleasant eventfulness. Day-to-day living is punctuated with elements of discord, the resolution of which calls for a striving on one's part. There is a functional element of inequality which is characteristic of all systems, be it marital or otherwise; and it is this inequality that provided the opportunity for the establishment of a nexus of trust between oneself and one's partner. Ideally, one can envisage a fifty-fifty relationship: but that is not life that is not marital reality. There is or should be a functional imbalance, the locus of which does not repose in one person but moves along a continuum of the two-party relationship. You love her and she loves you: and she will follow you in some ways and you will follow her in other ways. And it is your mutual trust and respect for each other that will provide the lubricant for this movement of initiative and thereby creating a living situation of equality.

There is no doubt that there are instances, as there will be when the preponderance of decision-making will repose on one party, not by virtue of that part's maleness or femaleness, but by virtue of the incidents that constitute the total complexity of the relationship. Factors that do play a part in this process are one's knowledge, ability, experience, and psychological temperament. But the thrust towards the assumption of any posture, regardless of how temporary, must, and for the survival of the marriage, be tempered with love, fairness, and wisdom. If there is communication on all levels of your relationship, and by this we not mean emotional academic duologues, then you all are on your way to constructing an edifice of some permanence. Like Rome, a marriage cannot be built in a day or a year. There will be difficulties and even traumatic encounters; but all these can be conquered for the greater part in the perseverance of your love.

It is indeed sheer folly to allow a relatively short period of dissension and perhaps disenchantment to have you turn your back on your marriage. The whole situation is like planting a garden of roses. Much sweat, labour, and annoyance are involved in this growing process; and before your roses can blossom in their pristine beauty, you will have been pricked by a thorn or two. In terms of your existential satisfaction and self-realisation, which is more significant, a bed of roses of your creation and of some durability, or artificial flowers picked up here and there in the course of your misguided philandering and temporary associations? The choice is yours. But our advice is this: once you have embarked on the marital voyage, hold on. It can be a very enchanting voyage despite the occasional billowing wave; and before this wave, you have the choice to hold on to each other in trembling though disturbing ecstasy; or vomit on each other's marital apparel. Again, the choice is yours. But again, we say that there will be difficulties as you both sail along, for such is life: in *rerum natura est* .

It has been stated that the first and seventh year of a marriage are the most critical in terms of marital breakdowns and separations. Keep this in mind and hold on to your marriage. It is yours and nobody else's; and any advice to give it up in the first two years of your marriage is in the vast majority of instances wrong. That is unless grave physical and psychological harm is imminent. We are in no way exhorting you to ensconce yourself in a situation that patently affects and inimically so, the development of the mysterious and beautiful dimensions of yourself. If there is a fundamental incompatibility in many areas of both your lives, and of which there should be a mutual acknowledgement, then it is wisdom to part despite an abiding sentimental concern.

As has been said, the most loving act is to allow another to go his or her own way. But this fundamental incompatibility must be there. It must be real: it must not be, as it can be a figment of your injured pride, misguided expectations, and delusions. Give yourself a chance: do things together and not merely meet the prosaic exigencies of your marital existence. Give yourself some time: for it is only in giving yourself some time, and in the context of the above, that you will be giving your marriage a chance.

Life can be, and most times is, problematic: and so any relationship at some point in its evolution will be problematic, and it will be left to you to ride the waves of your idealism and expectations with a strong will of pragmatism and realism. Beauty, it has been said, lies in the mind that contemplates: but the quality of that contemplation is predicated on the elements of reality which that mind, in its comparative function, perceives. But then what happens when the elements of that reality have been relegated to obscurity by virtue of factual incidents of living? Do you desist from contemplation and wallow mindlessly in a pool of life that has lost its distinctiveness, its uniqueness, by virtue of its pathetic Catholic inclinations? If you have given yourself some time, then a divisive course of action is warranted. The more idealistic one is, the more problematic a relationship will be, since the idealist dreams of what was – a certain innocence – and what could be. But the pragmatist lives in terms of what is. And so to meet the concrete exigencies of his situation, the idealist is torn apart by the wild bulls of contending thoughts and emotions. His only solace is himself, yet his torture chamber is his mind.

For the idealist, when there is an acute disjunction between what is and what one thought is, then a new reality, regardless of how morbid, comes into existence. The old and comforting reality is forever lost, as well as that part of himself that subsisted on what was. To what extent can an idealist compromise? Essentially, he cannot. He might try to attain a pragmatic, functional existence, which, of necessity, creates a dualism within the self. He becomes schizophrenic: he lives in two worlds, and the world he prefers is that which no longer is. In terms of his existential posture, life is absurd. But then he must deal with the elements of the concrete cocoon of his existence: and above all, he must maintain his sanity. And like Prometheus, who had his forever-growing heart clawed and tattered by the talons of his thoughts and his new reality, he must, within the silence of his being, sustain the universal rage of the cosmos – quietly.

Thus, we exhort you to be rational, understanding, pragmatic, mature, and loving. Give yourself and your relationship some time, some chance. If not, you may forever lose a pearl among the sands of your insensitivity, idealism, and immaturity. But if a parting of the ways is indeed inevitable, after all things have been considered and time given, take hold of yourself, particularly if there is still an abiding concern for the other. In the aftermath, you will find yourself tossed on a rather billowing sea of disappointments, contradictions, and paradoxes – all self- and other-oriented. The tidal pressure will be great and almost overwhelming: but somehow, you must survive this tragedy simply because you have to. Within yourself, you must find a port, a haven of security/serenity, of tranquillity. But then the storm subsists within and about you. But regardless of what, the rock to which you must cling can be found so that you can maintain your insanity in a state of functional equilibrium. It has been said that when it comes to pass, no sorrow is so great as we imagine it. There is truth in these words, and that perhaps could be your consolation. But our advice is this: be fair, be true, be manly, and be loving. If you are all of these very human things, then this situation of dissolution and despair will be grossly irrelevant to your marital situation. Bask in the sunshine of your relationship: that is the way it was meant to be.

A NOTION OF DEATH

Having dealt with some aspects of living, we think it of some significance to address ourselves to a seemingly unpleasant aspect of life; and that is death and dying. The purpose of our writing is to cause others to pause, ponder, and perhaps to act. And so in this regard, we have assumed the posture of the Socratic gadfly.

The **"beginning"** presupposes an **"end"**; and an "end" presupposes a "beginning". What is antecedent to the "beginning" is beyond us, and what is subsequent to the "end" is also beyond us. For that which is antecedent to the "beginning" falls into the realm of that which has no "beginning": and that which is subsequent to the "end" is that which has no "end". That which has no "beginning" and no "end" is the First and Supreme Principle of the cosmos: the Uncaused Cause: the Godhead. That which has a beginning and an end must, of metaphysical and logical necessity, emanate or spring from that which is greater than itself. The "beginning" is derivative of that which has no "beginning", and the "end" reposes in that which has no "end". The "beginning" is not the infinite, and so also is the "end". And so on an ontological level, the "beginning" and the "end" are becoming. Man, therefore, is "becoming". He is finite, and his beginning and end are incidents of his mortal existence.

From the pool of the infinite emerges that which is finite; and this emergence is cosmic benevolence translated in human terms. The circle as we know it is the most perfect of all forms. Now this emergence is part of the circle of divine love, and the other and vital part is the return to that pool of the infinite. Humankind has emerged from that pool of divinity, and thus its emergence finds its culmination in its reunion with its divine origin. And this reunion is effectuated through the instrumentality of the dying process. Without death, human life would be an absurdity, an impossibility since the project man would have lost its raison d'être and a certain cosmic thrust nugatory in its benevolent expression and manifestation. Assuming that there was no "end", no death, then the emergence and the subject of that emergence would be tantamount to being infinite. Man, therefore, would have to be God.

Man/woman are imperfect beings, and so the world they have created in its anthropological dimension must of necessity be imperfect; and it is that imperfection that provides in part the vital impulse for that movement towards the other side of the rainbow. There is an etiological nexus between man's imperfection and all that is good in his rather imperfect world: his morality, his laws, his philanthropism, his altruism, and religiosity. The equation on a very abstruse level is one of the biggest miracles of all and beyond time. As human evolution proceeds, as we are nearing the other side of the rainbow, we are partaking more and more of the intrinsic goodness of God. Man is not caught on a continuum of existence, at the poles of which are God and the Devil. The plenitude, the omnipresence, and omniscience of the former preclude the existence of the latter. In short, there is no Devil. It has been the figment of man's imagination from the beginning of time. Something conjured up to be used as a controlling agent and also to explain away the faults of man, and by so doing, transfer accountability for his misdeeds. And so in reiteration, there is no Devil, no hell-fire and no brimstone, and of course, no eternal damnation. For:

How can a finite being
In a finite situation
Commit a finite act
With finite deliberateness
And deserve infinite punishment?

We hold on to the proposition that an infinite act committed by a finite being is an impossibility. And so the ineluctable condition that can be arrived at is that death is without doubt not an infinite act or phenomenon interposed between the "beginning" and the "end". As far as human existence is concerned, the Alpha and the Omega, the "beginning" and the "end," birth, and death are subsumed under the rubric of that which is infinite, that which has no beginning and no end. That which is the Creator of the Omnicos.

And so the fear of death is unwarranted since death or the "end" is paradoxically a "beginning." The historical Jesus died on the cross allegedly to save mankind. From this it can be seen that associated with the very notion of death are the processes of saving and redeeming. And the question that can be asked is saving and redeeming for what and for whom. We do not believe that when a man effects his terrestrial demise that his body turns to dust and that his personality and vital essence are forever obliterated. We do not believe that the human subject that has and can demonstrate love, affection, sympathy, understanding, and goodness, that is able to perceive that which is beautiful and appreciate truth, and honesty, is destined to be the carrion for the maggots of the earth. Our belief is not a blind belief. On the contrary, it is rational and our faith is objective. It must be made quite pellucid that man is but a glimpse of the Creator and so his perception of that which is beyond him will be but a glimpse. Hence the faculty of faith should be rationally operative in the human subject and is an acknowledgment of his intrinsic limitations.

Through the keyhole of man's limited rationality, he can get a glimpse of that which is quintessentially rational and which exists quintessentially. And it is that glimpse that rationally calls upon the exercise of the faculty of faith. But the human appreciation of that which lies beyond the portals of death does not rest solely on human faith. Human rationality in conjunction with human faith, will, and can enable man to bridge the seeming hiatus between himself and that which is the essence of rationality – the Godhead. And it is he who stands waiting beyond the portals of death.

"I am not afraid of death, but I am afraid of dying". There are many for whom this statement of admission holds true. The abstraction of death does not frighten many; but the reality, the process, and immanence of death is frightening to a very large number. No one knows what it is really like at the critical moment, the last second of living, the appointed time: though we "die" every night in our sleep. The evidence seems to indicate that it is a moment of eventual release and tranquillity: a catharsis and then peace and tranquillity. Should that engender fear or is it the unknown? Perhaps the fear is not really the spectre of death or the dying process, but an awareness of what is being left behind. We are of the opinion that a great part of the fear consists of a concern for things incident to man's existence. And they are spouses, offsprings, loved ones, material wealth, and things attendant to that wealth. All this could be wrong. I think that it is the "unknown" and a certain uncertainty of a glimpsed certainty or reality.

Death is a gateway to that reality. It is a sublime communion of the Alpha and the Omega. It is a condition of life and for life.

SUICIDE

Considering the subject just discussed, we think it almost natural to articulate, however brief, on the related topic of suicide. Certainly, we are not inclined to the morbid; but then is suicide or death morbid?

In our culture and in many societies, the phenomenon of suicide as a moral act – moral from the point of view that it is a conscious act peculiar to man *qua* man - has the inquiring and socially perceptive mind addressing itself to a problematic situation. And it is a situation that encompasses two very profound questions: questions whose answers have great implications for man on a metaphysical and existential level. They are:

1. Is self-preservation the first law of life?
2. Is suicide an orientation towards life or death?

With regard to the first question, and if your answer were to be in the affirmative, who or what would have been the author of that principle? Would it be a principle that transcends the ontological situation of man as a rational entity, and thus making the will to love a condition of existing? In short, this principle of self-preservation would be a primordial condition of being characteristic of all existents – an epiphenomenon of being, a common denominator.

Such a view would preclude the concept, the notion, and the very actuality of suicide.

But man is not merely an existent: he falls into a special category that differentiates him from all other existents. He possesses a questionable faculty of rationality; he decides on the basis of experimental data and on things antecedent and immediate in his action space, and also on a futuristic projection of the past and present. He possesses a sense of perspicacity and he intends. He is a being with a rational faculty that has a power of choice. And it is a choice that is given significant expression by the posture that he assumes towards the enhancement of his life or on the contrary towards its seeming reduction to the unadulterated quintessence of nihility. For man this principle is not a blind ontological imperative since it is contingent on a quality of life that befits a rational human being. From this it can be seen that self-preservation and its antithesis are fundamental attitudes that, depending on one's existential situation and eschatological orientation, are given dynamic but exclusive expression. It is the issue of will and choice that brings in the element of moral worth or opprobrium in the situation of suicide. Our society has placed a very high premium – so it seems – on the sanctity of human life, which has been reinforced by religious dogma and doctrines. And hence all voluntary acts of self-annihilation have been considered as a monstrous travesty of this collective article of faith, and so have been condemned, however blindly.

Philosophically, behaviourally, and existentially, is that the right path: the correct tenet of faith?

When one considers the vagaries of human nature and the multiplicity of conflicting – in some instances- complexities that constitute man's attitudinal make-up, the phenomenon of suicide is not a simplistic and...

Voluntary determination of the will to die. Most suicided do not consider the flight from life as the supreme nullification of the self. To them, life is seen as something apart from the substantial life of the self: as though it were a state of affairs ancillary to the existence of the self: so that death is conceived as being instrumental in effecting a change from a finite and inhospitable situation to one that is above all tranquil and infinite: devoid of pain, anxiety , pathos, and failure. It is seen as putting an end to a stream of painful and temporarily contiguous events. Death is never construed as effecting the substantial demise of the self: and it is that qualified instrumentality that gives death its meaning of enticement. In short, and somewhat paradoxically, death is seen as having an instrumental value and not a terminal value.

Where is that principle of self-preservation as law?

Suicide is indeed the phenomenon that is peculiar to homo sapiens since the act is the product of a decision-making process. It is an option that is given dramatic expression in a universe of pathos, sometimes. The implication is that the individual intends the act of suicide and that his intention involves the concept and exercise of free will, and which is a reflection of the ego. But then when one thinks of the pathological-socio situation usually attendant to the theatre of suicide , the mutual anguish, pain, dilemmas experienced by some suicides (perhaps most) can the notion of free will, the autonomy of the ego, be particularly relevant. The question of ego autonomy is based on the question of action, which consists of three elements. They are (1) perception (2) interpretation (3) volition. To what extent can these three elements be operating on an optimal level in the individual who is demented and perhaps overwhelmed by morbid obsessions of failure, despair, and discovery? But are they all? We do hold that to embark on such a seemingly drastic course of action is sometimes a mindless quest for peace and tranquility. And do the mindless know that death, instinctively, is the gateway towards a desired end?

Isn't it possible that one could be lying in one's hammock at the Rudy John Beach Park in Laborie, with a glass of rum and coke in hand and with a smile take a deep drink knowing that his alcoholic beverage is laced with 70% arsenic? That is indeed very possible, my friend.

It was the venerable Roman Philosopher, Seneca, who posed this question. What is the end purpose of the good life? And across the silent legions of miles and into the centuries, Thomas Jefferson answered, "tranquillity". Beyond the portals of death, however circumstanced, stands awaiting the Price of Peace, the Author of Life. Suicide is an orientation towards Life and Death.

Having said all of this, the first Law of Life is not Self-preservation. Man is a rational, and equally so a social entity. And so for him, his first law of Life, which is indeed an existential imperative, is **Altruism**. The communion of the two raises on high, sublimates his very human attributes.

THE GENESIS OF EVIL

"In the beginning was the Word

And the word was with God

And the Word was God

The same was in the beginning with God

All things were made by Him".

(John 1:3)

T he questions that come to the fore are these: Did God create Evil, if all things were made by Him? Can Evil be created? Why would Evil be perceived as an exception in the celestial plenitude of the process of creating? According to biblical doctrine, the first allusion to this notion of Evil as a moving, conscious, and vibrant force was in the peculiar and incomprehensible metamorphosis of a celestial being called Lucifer: the first of the heavenly flock: the light of creation. According to Christian dogma, Lucifer was unblemished, a perfect being, seemingly endowed with a qualified attribute of immortality.

The demonic metamorphosis of Lucifer would seem to question the validity of this proposition: that which is the quintessence of perfection must, of logical and ontological necessity, produce only that which is tantamount to a phenomenon of its intrinsic and essential nature. In short, that which is perfect can only create that which is perfect. Is God perfect? Is God "is"? The resolution of the latter would propel us into certain dimensions of thought that would embrace the existential, ontological, teleological, eschatological, and cosmological. But that is another issue. As the biblical story goes, Lucifer became envious of the omnipotence of his creator – God. The celestial grandeur of Lucifer was not absolutely reflected in the created grandeur of Lucifer. There was a significant difference that engendered within the heart and mind of Lucifer that evil of envy. Lucifer certainly was not the author of his malediction: the equation of evil was not his creation. He was merely a factor of that creation.

In Isaiah 45:7, it states:

I form the light and create

The darkness. I make peace

And create calamity (evil)

I, the Lord, do all these things.

And so the question arises: was Lucifer a created calamity: a created Evil? In opposition, the question can be asked: was he created perfectly? If he were, then his descent into the abyss would not be possible. If he was perfect, and an attitudinal and characterological facsimile of God, then his thoughts, which more than any other aspect of his celestial composition would establish the nexus between himself and his Creator, and would evidence a functional and sublime salubriousness that would be the antithesis of the evil of envy. Logic would dictate that Lucifer was not created perfect, but he was created. The source of his Evil of Envy and its progeny cannot be attributed to him but to that which created him: his God.

Good and Evil: seemingly diametrically opposed constructs. Is God good and/ or is he Evil? Are both of these in their essence? Can the essence of Goodness and the essence of Evil repose in the same being? Is God an omni-cosmic composite? Perhaps that is where the answer lies. For to be God is to be quintessentially, absolutely, and eternally unlimited. To be constrained to the doing of Goodness eternally is an eternal limitation. The antithesis holds. God cannot be constrained to the doing of Evil eternally. A mutual exclusivity does not apply. But what really does not apply are the twin"human" conditions of Good and Evil. God is neither Good nor Evil. He simply is. He/She/It transcends the limits of man's comprehension and the adjectival interiorization of man and his *weltanschauung*. Good and Evil are human constructs that have no logical nexus with the attributes of God nor his existence. Good and Evil are theological necessities upon which is predicated the theological cosmology of mankind.

Man, as we know, is endowed with free will and therefore endowed with the faculty of choice. And the exercise of that choice can only validate the existence of that faculty in a very human scenario where

Good and Evil are constitutive elements in a universe of action. If we say and believe that God is omniscient, does that not make a mockery of the very notion of free will, and of man the jokers in some grand cosmic comedy? For it is the very notion of free will that gives relevance and validity to the very notion of free will.

As is to be noted, we do not believe in the many biblical pronouncements, declarations, and pontifications as being the word of God. As we see it in relation to the First Principle, the Uncaused Cause, Jesus/the Christ, the past, the present, and the future are one. And it is that notion of time that provides a situational relevance to the concept of Good and Evil just as it is time that makes possible the construct and materiality of "becoming". Man needs time. But for the Uncaused Cause, the First Principle, Jehovah, and the Godhead, there is no time. And so from an omnicosmological perspective, if there is no time, there is no Good and no Evil. But then has Good and Evil any relevance in the affairs of Man? The answer is Yes. Has it any relevance to the Uncaused Cause? The answer is no. And so there is no Judgement, no Hell-fire, no Heaven, and no Brimstone. There is just LOGIC.

A CERTAIN PERCEPTION

As has been indicated in certain sections of this book, Homo Sapiens are caught up in an evolutionary process. Perhaps to put it more accurately, man is the evolutionary process; for without him, evolution would be a cosmological absurdity. We believe that the genesis of his existence was in the form of an omnicosmic spark that had within it the germ of his human possibilities and, of course, his rationality. A spark derivative of the First Principle. And through the silent march of time, this spark, by virtue of its omnicosmic impulse, metamorphosed into various forms of being, until at a critical juncture in time, an organic entity with a manifest rational component came into being. Man, homo sapiens, had arrived. He possessed the requisite faculties for his continued evolution since his imperfections or deficiencies dictated that he evolve. At this point, the evolutionary process became his collective and individual responsibility. And so, as a rational being, he assumed the onus of accountability.

It is indeed true that Man is accountable for the further evolution of mankind, but he cannot be fully responsible for the expressed incidents of his limitations and imperfections in any situation of individual or collective judgement. Man must evolve: he must evolve to the point where he can legitimately be subsumed under the rubric of the Infinite. However, having reached this critical juncture by his own human energies, the leap into the abyss of the Infinite can only be made through the intervention of the Infinite, the Uncaused Cause. And this intervention of the Divine into the affairs of Man is called Love. And so, the nexus that binds the future with the Infinite is Love: an all-encompassing, all-knowing Love.

Considering the very grave dangers that threaten the existence of this finite being – atomic and nuclear explosions, climatic changes, just to mention a few – can it safely be assumed that the evolutionary process will continue without any calamitous disruptions? When we think of Man's greed ,his lust for power, his intransigence, his often-times blind nationalism, xenophobia in the light of nuclear arsenals of the super and mini powers, when we think of his imperfections ,his fallibility, and his myopia, we are inclined to conclude that a nuclear catastrophe is inevitable and that most of Man will be scorched off the face of this planet. In this regard, we should all keep in mind the terrifying fact that the Balkanization of the USSR. It has in its possession at least 5,000 nuclear warheads and 4,000 tons of biological material for weapons of mass destruction. Have all of this been accounted for? And it only takes one warhead on the shoulders of a demented individual or extraordinary, lucid terrorist to start a global conflagration. One individual whose tortured mind, evidencing a macabre distillation of his generational pain, his present frustration, and raging anguish, will couch the torment of his soul and mind in those words; "enough, is enough, is enough: so let loose the dogs of war".

Considering what presently obtains in Israel, Palestine, Afghanistan, North Korea, Russia, and China, and so forth, isn't it at least a probability, if not a certainty, that what we are alluding to could happen at any time – now? The law of averages and the peculiar history of Man with its progressive and regressive trends would seem to indicate the inevitability of this global catastrophe. And we believe that this tragedy of planetary proportions will occur within the next five hundred years. This, however, would not be the end. It cannot be since the project Man, by virtue of its extraordinary genesis, must be a success. To conclude otherwise would be to admit failure on the part of Man and level of the Godhead; and that is an impossibility.

Emerging from the miasma of nuclear wrath, "radiation man" will painfully grope upwards and towards his cosmic destiny. Post-nuclear man will be attitudinally, if not physically, different from pre-nuclear man, and it will be a change that will enhance the posture he assumes towards the attainment of his goal. The experience of his nuclear holocaust will purge him of his petty prejudices of race, religious ethnicity, culture, and nationalism. These are very divisive factors that were the cause of his nuclear experience. His emerging new world, characterised by the absence of these divisive elements, will and for the very first time facilitate the planetization of man: where the quality of the organic relation between man and his planet will evidence a wholesome and functional unity: a sublimating solidarity and symbolic global appreciation.

Matter, as it has been scientifically stated, cannot be destroyed. Energy is matter in a different form and therefore cannot be destroyed. All the energies expended by Man to reach that point in the evolutionary process are there around and about him. All the efforts expended, all the creative energies that have given rise to all forms of human achievement, are there, not wasted, not destroyed. And so Man, perhaps transformed by the radioactive influence of his nuclear experience, will have around and about him a pool of refined and creative energies from which to tap – consciously or subconsciously. The morality of Moses will not have been lost: the music of Beethoven will not be lost: the science of Einstein will not be lost, and the vision of Martin Luther King will not be lost. It will take post-nuclear man a far shorter period of time to reach the highest evolutionary point attained by pre-nuclear Man: his predecessors. And from there, human evolution will be moving full steam ahead, since a new collective awareness forged out of the fires of nuclear wrath will provide the vital thrust to the process of Man's evolution.

The nuclear conflagration will not only destroy Man and the physical incidents of his existence, but will also destroy the elements of division that have been a stumbling block in the convergence of this terrestrial universe and an etiological factor in that doomsday confrontation. When examined most profoundly and critically, it would seem that one of the most critical elements of division and confrontation has been culture. The multiplicity of cultures that are attendant to the myriad geographical groupings of Man is at this point in time an impediment to his further evolution of Man. As we see it, cultural pluralism or diversity must become obsolete for it is essentially dysfunctional in this theatre of human evolution. And it is only through the fires of nuclear wrath/war of mass destruction that the obsolescence of culture will be effectuated and replaced by a world culture: the homogenisation of cultures. As the evolutionary process proceeds rather inexorably towards its intended goal, the universe of Man is slowly but surely moving in on itself. Man and systems are beginning to find themselves in the embrace of each other; and so in a way and on a somewhat limited scale, the homogenisation process has begun and which will be accelerated and consummated by nuclear wrath. And this centripetal movement is being evidenced at this time on a political, economic, demographic, and societal level.

Today we allude to the phenomenon of globalisation, which is yet to be perceived as a secular process. It is essentially spiritual in its intent, purpose, and scope. And though at this time the emphasis seems to be on the economic, man must move towards the globalisation of politics, culture, religion, and law. In spite of or despite himself, man is indeed caught in the embrace of other men. Modern information communication technology, rapid means of travel, the wars around the globe, the refugees from diverse places, devastation by floods, and so forth, all these phenomena or events are contributing to this universal and terrestrial convergence and planetisation of man. What in this day and age of limited vision is regarded as the mongrelisation of the races will, in the fullness of time, one thousand years hence, be viewed in an entirely different light. That is, in an era of post-nuclear man. All the barriers of apartheid, of whatever the stripe, will be broken down and sanitised; and that abominable stratagem that does violence to the human spirit will in time be relegated to the trash-heap of historical oddities.

The ongoing Civil Rights Movement and other related social thrusts with their sublime and ideal visions are now being inculcated in the conscious and subconscious minds of this and coming generations – regardless of how slowly. The isolation of China is presently being whittled away, and the Eastern bloc is multi-metering its way across the turbulent waters of a regimenting ideology to a vibrant and accommodating West. In this regard, one can keep the European Union in mind. And from a very regimenting and regimented society (there have been some recent democratic changes), we have a Pope, the head of a universal spiritual movement. The cultural dilution or adulteration is on its way, and by an eclectic process, the best of what is essentially human will provide a milieu for the birth of the Universal Man. Unfortunately, he will be post-nuclear Man. When man emerged from the ooze of his animalization, there was indeed a need for the many diverse cultures. The integrity of man qua man could only be attained and sustained in relatively small groupings which were facilitated by man's ethnic, racial differences, and geographical distances. But now man strides across the earth like a colossus: and it is his right to do so. The integrity of his essential self is beyond question, and this has been and is reflected in the morality of his many systems. Homo Sapiens: he stands supreme in his integrity but situationally divided. What then is the next evolutionary step/leap?

From the ashes of a nuclear holocaust, a philosophy of a Universal Humanism embracing and directing an evolving entity that will be neither African, American, British, Asian, European, Chinese, and so forth. He will merely be the Universal Man. And unlike pre-nuclear man, his very integrity and dignity will be predicated on the basis of his possibilities and potentialities. The future will be his guiding star rather than his past and history. By gazing at, and striving for that which lies beyond himself, the Universal Man will have transcended his ancestors' myopic obsession with their roots. The Universal Man will be essentially defined in terms of what he can be and not in terms of what he was. A corollary to this extraordinary emergence will be the nullification of all political world systems as we know them. The Universal Criterion will be: are you a "Man"; and the operating philosophy and principle will be Love, Human Brotherhood, and Human Solidarity. The Universal Man will transcend all pseudo and petty constraints of politics, ethnicity, race, religion, economics, and culture. At this time, he will have taken a major step in his evolution. By the year 3023 AD, all this will come to pass. How many of us in this so-called enlightened world can and will perceive the celestial vision of a thousand years?

Where does all of this put the West Indian? At this time, we see him as a primordial prototype of the Universal Man. Unfortunately, he has not yet been able to see his place in omnicosmic history. He is still shackled by the constructs of cultural diversity and cultural myopia. But of all of the races, he is ideally placed to be the first of the Universal Man.

A PERCEPTION OF BLACKNESS

Black is Beautiful!

But is black more beautiful than brown, yellow, or white? And if it is indeed beautiful, then one question that can be asked is to whom? If black is beautiful only to blacks, then a certain vital consensus is lacking, which militates against the universality of this laudable proposition and subverts teleological existentialism of being black.

We do not subscribe to the notion that black is more beautiful than brown, yellow, or white. However, it is of vital importance that he who is black must believe in the intrinsic pulchritude of his blackness in order to appreciate, identify with, and relate in a rather wholesome manner to those who are brown, yellow, or white. In other words, the black man must first be able to love himself most authentically before he can love that which is other than black; he must be able to revel in the pulchritude of his negritude. But this posture assumed in terms of his blackness must, of necessity, be a function of his profound belief in his intrinsic worth as a man.

Being a man is substantive, and being black is qualitative. And so ideally, there should be a salubrious attitudinal and relational nexus between the substantive and the qualitative. Now, this belief in his essential worth cannot be fostered in a vacuum, nor can it be engendered within the heart of the black man as he stands, regardless of how majestically in a cauldron of seething bigotry and hate. Because of the very quiddity of man, he can only love if he has been loved: and therefore, a certain particular and collective responsibility devolves upon his fellow man to participate in his human evolution and spiritual development.

From our perception, the phenomenon of slavery and colonialism was tantamount to a crass prostitution of very elementary human ethical principles, and were in their various expressions of domination and exploitation a brutal and callous abdication of that particular and collective responsibility. In consequence thereof, the black man was not only deracinated but dehumanised. He was dehumanised, but up to a point. In the swirling waters of colonial hate, racism, and bigotry, he was buffeted. On the reefs of Europe's greed, he was mangled. And as he lay gasping on the torturing plantations of his island habitats, his very being was assaulted by the seeming instrumentality of his blackness.

As he looked with bloodied eyes through the keyhole of his miserable circumstance, he saw in the mirror placed beyond a reflection of a distortion. The substantive and qualitative were distorted; the authentic relational hiatus was deliberately blurred since he was not told that the mirror was cracked. And as he in time struggled across the arena of his mirrored existence, he was confronted at each step and on every level by the three-dimensional image of his existence: his perception of himself, his society's perception of himself, and his perception of society's perception of himself. A trinity of misperceptions. Then bombarded by a faith quite alien to his very cosmology and which made him assume even more a posture of submission , and then relegated to the basest stratum of a socio-economic hierarchy, he was coerced into believing that his situation of degradation was in the natural order of things – in *rerum natura est* – simply because he was black; and that his seeming humanity was an acquired trapping by virtue of his pathetic association with what seemed essentially human and white.

Unlike the Jews, the Black man was always considered subhuman; and so that essential human dignity which the Jews could courageously display even in their macabre setting, even before the showers of Auschwitz, was to an appreciable extent smothered by the blanket of slavery and colonialism. It is our opinion that if Hitler had won the war, the Jews would have been liquidated as a people; but the Blacks would have fared far worse; theirs would have been a living hell, a living death; they would have been made slaves in mind, body, and soul since their very essence would have been quintessentially denied. In the showers of Auschwitz, the Jews, at least, and as a people, had a grotesque sense of dignity.

All that is human is rational. All men are human; therefore, all men are rational. And so to the extent that one deviates from the expression of his rationality, then to that degree he ceases to be human, he ceases to be man or man-like. Being human, being man is the actualisation of a certain divine cosmic potentiality that inures within the very core of the being and existence of homo sapiens. In the womb of Africa, this potentiality was actualised; and the Black man as he walked majestically away from the Olduvai Gorge stood tall in the sure and certain knowledge that he shared a sublime kinship with the First Principle of the Universe, and that in relation to the living world around him, there devolved upon him a certain responsibility that had to be discharged within the context of his innate benevolence and rationality. He was Man. He was Human. He was Rational. And the incidents of his rational humanism were given profound expression in the societies of love, justice, respect, and honour that he created. And so for thousands of years, between and among the oak trees of Africa, and along the Nile and Zambezi rivers, and on the shores of the Indian and Pacific Oceans, he the Black man lived and died in dignity.

And so it was a man, a man in the full dignity of his manhood that was immolated on the cross of "enlightened" Europe's economic salvation and that endured the opprobrium of slavery. That which was and is human was dehumanised – but up to a point. For within the deepest core of his being, the Black man in pain, in anguish and in torment, in his particular situation of existential pathos, drew upon the well-springs of his humanity and sublimated in part, through song, his grotesque situational posture.

Like Sisyphus, he carried the rock of his degradation up and along the hill of his very human aspirations; but unlike the blinding compulsion of the former, he was motivated by a sometimes articulated and sometimes unarticulated desire to be free. And so for generations upon generations, the Black-man and as a people, raised himself by dint of hard work unsurpassed in the annals of human endeavours, raised himself on all levels of his existence, up and from his situation of physical, moral and characterological degradation. It was a struggle. It is a struggle. For though his material acquisitions and intellectual and academic achievements may reflect a certain victory for himself, and a certain conquest over his oppressors, yet the trauma of his collective experience has left him in his generality, scarred on significant and interior levels of his being. From a chasm of social bondage, from a pit of educational bondage, from a mire of psychological bondage and from a vice of economic bondage, he the Black-man had to extricate himself. And this he did and is doing through the instrumentality of his indomitable spirit. For him, there never was, nor could be, spiritual bondage.

And it was this spirit in its action-oriented manifestations that tugged upon the hearts and dormant sensibilities of the generally debased other. And it was this subsequent cooperation in the circumstance of humanity that has enabled and in enabling that generalised other to remove itself from the morass of bigotry, hypocrisy, and ethical infantilism in which it wallowed. Yes, the Black man was mutilated and debased. But that was only one part of the equation. That generalised other was also debased and mutilated: for he who debases and mutilates another is already himself debased and mutilated. And so this subsequent situation of cooperation in the circumstance of humanity was, and is making abundantly clear, that however disparate our genetic endowments, however different the pigmentation of our epidermis, we are still human beings who share the same human aspirations, conditions, and limitations, and are therefore linked - ontologically, eschatologically, existentially - by these facts.

However, it must be noted by the Black man that the millennium has not yet arrived. He therefore must be very vigilant and forever striving to realise himself, not just by himself, since only a partial realisation can be attained, but in concert with the brotherhood of Man. He must be open in his thinking and in his perceptions, but yet be forever vigilant since his history has indicated in no uncertainty that while it is true that Man is higher than the beasts, it is also equally true that he has powers to sink below them.

He, the BLACK MAN, must have faith in the ultimate goodness and rationality of the community of men; but he must have faith in himself. He must be able to revel in the pulchritude of his negritude; **but above all, he must be proud of himself as a MAN.**

LAW, JUSTICE & LIBERTY

Human beings are creatures of imperfections and, as a consequence of their intrinsic flaws, which manifest themselves on at least a moral and characterological level. There have always been individuals prone to doing violence to human life and inadvertently inclined to transgress the rights and privileges of others. And it is as a result of this tyranny, using the term rather broadly, that society has seen it fit to enact and codify laws to guarantee and to safeguard the rights and freedom of the individual and the generalised other. The law is the codification and institutionalisation of the mores of a group in the context of proscription and prescription. It is an indispensable dimension of the societal phenomenon; for without a concept of order and of discipline, a society could never come into existence. For society implies order, discipline: it implies Law.

So law consists of rules limiting the freedom, or more accurately, curtailing the propensity to license of individuals and groups. However, as regards the quiddity of law, attention must be focused on the notion of Justice. And it is purely in the context of a terminal value that law essentially obtains its d'être as an instrumental value. And it is the universal need for Justice, which is imbued with an element of self-preservation and hence enlightened self-interest, that has given rise to a system of law: that has made of law a functional sub-system of every society, be it tribal or technological.

Since the legal powers of governmental authorities with respect to societal liberties have been codified in legal tomes and usually couched in an esoteric jargon or terminology incomprehensible to the layman, and also since these codifications are indeed capable of diverse interpretations, it has been necessary for the State to provide a forum for the interpretation and comprehension of these laws, as they apply to the mundane affairs of society. And this process of interpretation in the context of the layman's needs is carried out through the instrumentality of legal counsellors: the lawyers.

The generality of law is for the most part known to the layman. But then, the layman is not confronted by general legal problems. His problems are specific and deserving of specific legal solutions. And it is his awareness of the legal specificity of his problem with its attendant specific consequences that induces him to seek legal aid or assistance. And it is on this level that law, as seen through the eyes of the layman, is regarded as a body of abstruse, abstract, incomprehensible principles. Thus his only recourse is to the lawyer whose specialised and uncommon knowledge places him in the ideal situation to help or, in some cases, exploit his client's reliance. And it is this helplessness which incidentally generates feelings of distrust that force the layman to assume a somewhat ambivalent posture towards his "saviour" or potential "tyrant".

Much has been done through professional codes of conduct to mitigate the ambivalence and to raise on high and to maintain on some dignified level, the practice of law. But regardless of what, in the final analysis, the probity of the lawyer's conduct and dealings with his client, rests with the lawyer. And so, the climate of distrust and suspicion prevails, since in the fabric of the past, the layman can discern regardless of how infrequent, threads of professional violence and financial rape. Caveat emptor: let the buyer beware. And so the layman must be protected: and interestingly enough so also the lawyer. There must be sanctions: and the parameters that must be drawn in terms of sanctionable conduct must of necessity evolve from the definitional expectations and perceptions inherent in the term professional. For the lawyer is a professional. And now the question arises, what does the term professional mean? As we envisage it, the term professional connotes an individual with a functional level of expertise and who as such operates within the parameters of a code of conduct that transcends the individual's occupational life. It implies the assumption of a philosophical posture in terms of one's *modus operandi* and *modus vivendi*. And so any canon of ethics for the lawyer, for the professional, must of necessity address itself to the total behaviour of that class of persons.

The key word that constitutes the foundation of any code of ethics is "integrity": and integrity implies wholeness and wholesomeness.

There is no question of partial probity. The lawyer does not cease being a lawyer when he divests himself of his legal apparel, his robes: just as a surgeon does not cease being a surgeon when he removes his surgeon's gloves. Though it might be said that a legal code of ethics constitutes in some respect an invasion of privacy by virtue of its sanctionable and non-sanctionable demands and expectations, yet on a very abstruse level such an obtuse and artificial opinion has no meaningful validity; since being a lawyer and being a professional is an honourable extension of the quiddity of man as a rational being. His professionalism is his philosophy in operation and his philosophy is the existential expression of his being. In other words and in the language of the ancients, *SUM QUOD FACTO*: I am what I do.

We shall at this juncture address ourselves to the notion of Justice since the law and the practice of law are intimately entwined with this terminal value. The term justice has been used in a multiplicity of situations and in a multiplicity of forums. The plebeians cry out for Justice and the patricians maintain that they have dispensed Justice. And so what is this Justice that seems to be the object of universal concern? What is Justice? Is it the figment of a rather fecund Hellenic imagination: a mirage on the desert of Law? Or is it a value that transcends Man that is above him and yet paradoxically not essentially beyond him? It is, however, through the instrumentality of Law that Man can in some ways attain a pragmatic functional approximation to this value within the parameters of his intrinsic limitation.

It must pellucidly be understood that whereas Law is a product of human reason, Justice is not. In terms of the human subject, it is a condition of "being"; it is a *sine qua non* for the further evolution of the human species. It is a universal imperative in terms of which a particular species can maintain and attain its particular and omnicosmic destiny. Thus every rational being possesses what may be termed a natural sense of Justice – *vulgaris aequitas*. And this sense of Justice is a function of man's rationality. He who ceases to be rational ceases to have a sense of Justice. Now when one addresses oneself to the fact of the human condition, it becomes patently clear that Man is not essentially a rational being. If he were, we would not be thinking of the bathos of human existence when certain historic happenings are brought to mind, and the pathos of human experience. The macabre waltz of the Palestinians and Israelis is a case in point.

Man, however, does possess a rational faculty as well as other faculties. Besides the rational, there are other dimensions to his person; and if in a moment of misguided pretension of his worth, we conclude that he is rational, then it can be said and justifiably so, that he is equally irrational. However, it is through this principle of rationality – despite its imperfect manifestation within the human frame – that man becomes cognisant of the need for a pragmatic functional expression of Justice in order to meet the exigencies of his societal existence, the unarticulated need of his collective evolution, his ontology, and his eschatological apprehensions and postulations, regardless of how dubious. And thus, it can be seen that man's rationality in its manifest sense of Justice establishes the nexus between what is quintessentially terminal and what is from a metaphysical perspective "becoming".

And so again we pose the question: What is Justice? When strictly construed, perhaps it can be said that Justice definitionally can be couched in this biblical phrase: "**an eye for an eye, a tooth for a tooth**". But that of course is a rather simplistic definition of the term; for no two eyes are the same, and the significance placed on the eye and its functions may differ from individual to individual. If one's eye is removed by another, is it Justice to remove in turn the eye of the other who happens to be a one-eyed man? Or is it just to remove in turn the astigmatised of the two-eyed other for the loss of one's good eye?

Perhaps it can be said that Justice is the rendering of what is due or merited. But then, on what basis does one make that decision? What yardstick can be used to measure in strict equitable terms a man's merit or his just deservings? The answer to this could be a moral principle by which actions are determined as right and just.

What then are the implications of this answer? Since we are speaking of Justice in terms of man *qua* man, then the assumption must be made that this moral principle is catholic in its implication and derivative of a universal frame of reference. But then when we think in terms of morals, moral deeds, moral actions, we think in terms of actions that befit man as man. One cannot ascribe "moral" as a prefix to any action or activity to an entity that is not human. It is only in terms of the human subject that the term moral has any relevance and significance. Now the question arises, what is the conduct that is befitting man as man? Different cultures and different civilisations at different and contemporaneous times have given different answers to that question. What one culture has considered right, just, and proper, has been condemned, castigated in another. The conclusion is that there is no such thing as a universal frame of reference: certainly not at this juncture in time. Situational ethics come to mind. If one's thinking is further extended, then the seemingly logical inference that must be made is that in terms of the human condition, Justice can only partially and subjectively be realised. And the degree of realisation is a function of the degree of human evolution.

In our society, Justice is deemed to be obtained through the instrumentality of the legal system: and of which the Law is the codification of certain moral principles alluded to earlier. And the Law, we say, is just and equitable: no one is above the law. And so, the Law in its majestic equality is applied to unequal persons in varying and different circumstances. As a matter of pure logic, if the equal is applied to the unequal then the result must be "in" or "un" equality. And "in" or "un" equality is certainly not Justice. As we said earlier, man can only approximate to this construct of Justice, which eventually is an attribute of the Supreme Principle and cannot really be compartmentalised. One can make arbitrary decisions for convenience, but they hold no basis in reality.

Hence Justice is Love, is Fairness, is Compassion, is Order - on our level. And all of these factors are constitutive elements of one's rationality. Because of Man's innate weaknesses and insalubrious propensities, we have seen doctrines of pragmatism and convenience substituted for Justice. Man is human and so his conceptions can only be human as well as his achievements. He is imperfect and thus his achievements must be less than perfect. Can the imperfect being attain perfect Justice? No! And since he is not the author of his own creation, then any Supreme Being must take cognisance of his limitations in any perceived situation of judgement. If that is indeed relevant and necessary.

Throughout his terrestrial sojourn, Man, by virtue of his possibilities and ongoing evolution, will endeavour to bridge the hiatus between his expression of Justice and that which is quintessentially just. It is a subjective but global movement actuated by a philosophy of a Universal Humanism. Justice cannot be a tit-for-tat affair: there are too many variables in the individual's action space for the human mind to encompass and consider. Also, man is not responsible for his genetic make-up, which may be the basis for certain criminogenic proclivities. And so Justice on our rather human level must be a human expression of love, of fairness, of compassion, and of order. And it is only a being that possesses a rational faculty that can so manifest. Through the keyhole of our rather human circumstance, we have been able to get a glimpse of the elusive Goddess of Justice – Themis. But then we know how far a lover will go in search of the being he is enamoured with, how much further then will a lover of Justice go in search of his Divine Mistress.

We shall now at this juncture move into the last of the three verities: Law, Justice, Liberty. When one addresses oneself to the concept of Liberty, one immediately finds oneself caught up in a morass of conflicting notions. Does the term Liberty imply or connote freedom? And if so, isn't freedom the power and perhaps the right to do as one pleases? Can this be an unequivocal definition of these two in light of this interesting notion, licence? Can it not be said that the above enunciated elaboration of the terms freedom and liberty does not meet the definitional requirements of the word licence? How can one draw a meaningful line of demarcation between liberty and licence? On what level can one perceive an essential and crucial dichotomy? We do not think that the answer lies in the realm of etymology.

When we think of the liberty of the human subject, we must address ourselves to human behaviour, human conduct, and human finitude. There may be something called infinite liberty, but we believe that it would be rather asinine on our part to postulate a notion of infinite liberty within the context of a very finite situation. And so, to hold on to that notion in the face of the ethical ramifications of that concept would be tantamount to a bathos of absurdity. Its speculative operational consequences as we envision it would lead to a prostitution of human life. Infinite liberty may repose in some omnicosmic principle – God. But though Man may aspire to be God, though he may have delusions of being God, he most certainly is not God.

Again, we refer to the former question: on what level can a gap be perceived between liberty and licence? In our judgement, we believe that it is on the level of the ethical that a significant differentiation can be made. With regard to the definition that has so far been articulated, that is, the power and the right to do as one pleases, it can be seen that liberty embraces two cardinal components: power and right. And it is the question of right that brings in the element of ethics into the concept of liberty. It can further be seen that there are two fundamental principles in the very notion of liberty. They are possession of a self-determining power and the condition of being ethically free. And it is this principle of ethics that forces us to hold on to the proposition that liberty must be restricted in order to be possessed. And it is also this principle that induces us to postulate that the basis of morality is liberty.

As we alluded earlier, liberty can only be envisaged in terms of human behaviour, human conduct. And when this conduct is superimposed upon a continuum in man's respective action space, we see at one polar region the brute reality of licence and at the other the subversive reality of regimentation or servitude. Between these two poles, we have gradations of human conduct: and liberty is the mean between these two extremes. Licence focuses itself on the issue of an atavistic power and relegates to some moral abyss the issue of right. As we all know, an ethical being can make choices, but among the plethora of choices he is confronted with and all those activities, he, as an ethical being, cannot entertain them in a theatre of action. Hence, the very notion of liberty implies the notion of restrictions. If that power and right to do as one pleases were not curtailed, man would be creating an unhealthy situation, which in no uncertain terms would do violence to the human spirit and ideal. Man would be creating an environment in which every man would be giving vent to his lascivious inclinations and cupidity. It would be a world of anarchy, a world of chaos. And so in relation to Man, the ideal situation, the ideal posture is that golden mean between those two extremes. It must be a posture in consonance with the very quiddity of man's fragilities, his imperfections, and his finitude. Reiterating the above definition, liberty is the power and the right to do as one pleases. In a societal context, a corollary of every right is a duty. The very fabric of our society is made up of rights and duties; and to remove one structural, one functional element would amount to granting to ourselves something akin to unlimited freedom, unlimited liberty; and this would be tantamount to setting loose upon ourselves the malevolent designs of the unscrupulous and morally bankrupt. From this, it can be seen that in having unrestricted liberty, we as Man essentially do not have liberty.

What is the purpose of Liberty? As we see it, the purpose of liberty is the realisation of ourselves as men. Can we realise ourselves, our potentialities in a situation of chaos – a situation of anarchy? If men were Gods, then the question of unlimited liberty would not be problematic. Can man, on the other hand, realise himself in a situation of servitude? The answers are indeed patently clear. The very existence of our society, of our institutions, is indeed testimony of the approximate realisation of ourselves as men; and that undoubtedly is tied to the fact that we as men have exercised a restricted liberty and which essentially is liberty in human terms. To remove restrictions – and they are the duties, normative constraints upon us by our society and the anticipations of our fellow system members – we as men would in truth and in fact be slaves and victims of our primal propensities.

Destitute of liberty, we would regress to the level of sophisticated human animals.

GENESIS REVISITED

From the onset, we would like to state quite categorically that we do not subscribe to the notion or theory of Special Creation; and so our cosmological view is diametrically opposed to the biblical postulation of Genesis. As we see it, Genesis exemplifies the limits of human imagination and knowledge at a particular point in time. The writers of Genesis relied on the physical evidence of their senses in order to create a world and worldview – *weltanschauung* – that would be in conformity with the normative expectations and anticipations of the general body of knowledge that existed at that time. To have written that the sun revolved around the Earth and that the Earth was one of many planets would have been sheer lunacy devoid of any intervention by a God, however defined. That brings to mind the Galilean/Paola/ Christian controversy in the 1600s AD.

As we see it, there is nothing in the Genesis narration that evidences the intervention of a God in a manner and to a degree that conforms with the scientific discoveries made throughout the effluxion of time. Why didn't the God of Moses give him and subsequent generations an insight into the complexity of the universe? What Genesis palpably discloses is the vastitude of human ignorance at that time, and the biblical writers' attempt to create a cosmology that would validate their existence and reason for having embarked on a simple, as opposed to sophisticated. and for us now, a simplistic creation of their world. It is a creation that does not do justice to that which is quintessentially magnificent and omnificent.

To us, the Book of Genesis is like a fairy tale and does not in any way reflect the sublime majesty of an omnicosmic Creator. Why create a world in "six" days when for the Uncaused Cause time did not exist? Has six or seven days any special ultra-terrestrial significance? Why create Adam out of the muck of the earth? Was that to ground his being in what was essentially physical? Why create Eve out of the rib of Adam and thereby, and from the very beginning, instituting the notion of inequality between the sexes? Incidentally, at the time of Moses, inequality between the sexes was normative: a way of life. How many wives did the "associates" of God have?

At this juncture, we shall studiously address ourselves to the Book of Genesis, make our observations, and arrive at our various conclusions. Between verses 1-19, the God of Moses, who henceforth we shall refer to as God, created the organic and inorganic world in some measure. In verse 1, it reads in part: **In the beginning, God created the heaven and the earth.** And that beginning could only be in terms of what was created since it is the act of creation that introduces the notion of time, which we see as an epiphenomenon of creation. The first two entities that were created were the heaven and the earth, which were formless and empty. The question that now arises is how the earth could be formless, since as an entity, and of ontological necessity, it must have parameters to establish its unique existence – its beingness. The second verse continues with darkness being upon the face of the deep, and the spirit of God moving upon the face of the waters. We are inclined to associate the "deep" with "waters" and that the spirit of God, which as we see it is one and the same entity as God.

Then in what would have been Stygian darkness, God introduced in some measure the "light," which in further measure displaced a portion of the eternal darkness. The Light he called Day, and the darkness Night. All of this took place on the first day of creation, which consisted of the evening and the morning. Rather perplexing. That is sheer human imaginings. Since he moved upon the waters, where did the waters come from? Obviously, it was created out of nothing. But then he is God.

In the second phase and act of creation, God brought into existence the firmament, which divided the waters and thus formed a body of water above and another below. The firmament, from our understanding, is a vault, an orb. God called the firmament heaven. Above that firmament or heaven, there should be another body of water. Was that according to the Mosaic body of knowledge or an indirect, simplistic explanation of rain falling from the sky? All of this concluded the second phase and act of creation.

In the third phase and act of creation, and under the firmament of heaven, God created the sea by gathering the waters in one place. By so doing, the land appeared. The question that comes to the fore is this: where was the dry land before the "gathering of the waters"? Or was the land always there, since in verse one it states: **In the beginning, God created the heaven and the earth.**

Having gathered the waters, which obviously was above the land, that land was called earth, and the gathered waters were called the sea. Was there one sea or several seas?

God then ordered the earth to fructify in various ways and modes, and thus giving rise to what generally has been described as flora or plant life. In the next act or phase of creation, he brought into existence the various lights in the heavens to facilitate the natural divisions of the seasons, days, nights, and years, and while so doing, he created as special, luminous orbs: the sun and the moon. "And God set them in the firmament to give light upon the earth". The sun and the moon predominantly provide light during the day and night, respectively. There is no information pertaining to their size, their composition, their distance from each other, and their distance from the Earth. Nothing scientific was disclosed since that knowledge during mosaic times was not available and could not be ascertained by man.

The fifth act and phase of creation gave rise to diverse marine life and to the birds that flew beneath the canopy of heaven. It would seem that the fowl population emerged from the waters. Also, in this phase, all non-marine animal life was created. The verse reads: "let the earth bring forth the living creature after its kind...".

In the last and sixth phase and act of creation, God created man. Genesis reads: "Let **us** make man in our image, after our likeness...". A concern that arises is, what is meant by "us"? Does it imply plurality or was this word used in the mode of the royal we and therefore signifying singularity? We are inclined to opt for the latter. In verse 27 it reads: "And created Man in his own image, the image of God created he him: male and female he created them". This verse we find very interesting and perplexing. What really was meant "in his own image"? Already one perceives a distancing between the Creator and the creature; and it is a distancing on a quintessential substantive level. Since God is spiritual his image has to be less than spiritual, but it must be in some measure a repository of some attributes that God enjoys. Being in the image cannot be in terms of the physical but in terms of his possibilities, potentialities and divine expectations.

Whereas God is Being, man is Becoming. He has certain possibilities which is the reflection on the image of God. Continuing with verse twenty-seven (27) it reads: "...in the image of God he created him male and female created he them." In this sixth day of creation, did God create man and woman at one and the same time, or did he first create Man? In the previous phases and acts of creation contemporaneity or instantaneousness were features of God directive. But as regards Man male or female, was there a separation in time? Provide the answer: or do they?

On the seventh day, as indicated in Chapter 2 verse 2, God rested. The question that arises is why would God rest, since God, as conceptualised is the quintessence of benevolent energy? Again, one sees very human conditions, human perception, human experience and human expectations. And again one sees the limits of human experience.

In verse seven (7) there seems to be Man – the male. The verse reads as follows:

"And the Lord God formed Man of the dust of the ground, and breathed into his nostrils the breath of life, and Man became a living soul."

Is this a second act of the creation of Man and is it the mundane mechanics of the first act of creation? We are of the opinion that this was a further elucidation of the first act of creation. And so, the male was created before the female. After having created the man, God created the Garden of Eden, and in that garden he "grew" a multiplicity of trees pleasant to the senses; and in their midst he grew the Tree of Life and the Tree of Knowledge of Good and Evil. Two very special trees. And in that garden he placed the man to maintain and cultivate them as well as the other trees and plants.

What we find intriguing in relation to verse (8) is this: It reads: "And the Lord God planted a garden eastward in Eden..". One quite logically must conclude that Eden is a place, and it is a place as distinct from other places. How did Eden come about? Did God embark on a demarcation exercise, and if so, for what reason? There is only one man, one human being on Earth. Again, one becomes aware of the human limitations of the mosaic writers. All that they wrote was within human parameters; and so, they depicted the state, level, and extent of their cognitive abilities at that time.

By the way, what became of the Garden of Eden? Having placed Man in the garden situated in Eden, God then directed him not to eat of the fruit of the Tree of Knowledge and Good and Evil, and that should he so disobey, he would die. At this point in his development, did Adam know the meaning of "death and dying"? What is interesting to note is that it is God who imports the notion of Good and Evil into the world of Man. And so, the question that comes to mind is how is this possible if God is indeed the quintessence of that which is Good.

And the diabolicalness of it all is that Man is endowed with free will. Why warp the very notion of creation by introducing the element of Evil in whatever form or mode? Why not create a magnificent garden reflective of his own ineffable magnificence? Why introduce death and dying in this newly created world? Being omniscient, he knew that man at some time would disobey. He knew that man was imperfect and liable to err. But then, as we see it and on an ontological level, it is a metaphysical impossibility for that which is the quintessential of perfection to create an entity that is imperfect. Since, and paradoxically so, and within the very corpus of God would repose an element of evil or imperfection. That would be logically offensive, outrageous, and ludicrous.

Following from this is the notion of Death. Did Man know the meaning of death, the significance of death in all of its implications and ramifications? Did death mean for him the cessation of all human activities: of all life; that on whatever level he would cease to exist? That he, the man, would be unable to partake in and to enjoy his paradisiacal terrestrial circumstance? Death was the ultimate, definitive, eternal punishment. It was categorically existential and there seems to be no reprieve.

Disobey and die. It was a loss of the joys of Eden, the loss of life, and loss of his proximity to God. There was no forgiveness, which in our opinion, is the highest expression of Love: forgiveness that encompasses the unrepentant. One further needs to ponder on the "Tree of Life", what is its significance? What does it play in the life of man? Why wasn't this a divine prohibition?

After some lapse of time, it seemed to have dawned upon God that the man was in need of a companion. That thought or awareness was antecedent to the creation of the man, otherwise the creation of man and woman would have been contemporaneous. And verse 18 reads: "And the Lord God said, it is not good that Man should be alone: I will make a helpmate for him."

All of this is human thinking, human experience: all of this is being human. And so now, the Man who is called Adam is in need of a helper – not a companion since that implies meeting an emotional need; and it is reflective of the man-woman relation in those times. Adam's job was to maintain and cultivate the garden. By the way, who named him Adam?

Then woman is created and the mechanics of it all is covered by verses 21 and 22, which disclose a highly and ungodly ineffable process. If Adam was asleep when he was "de-ribbed" and the woman formed, how did he know the details of the process?

Whatever, the woman is now present in the life and world of Adam, whom he calls woman. They were both naked and oblivious to their nudity. Should they be aware of their nakedness since they had no frame of reference? Then the woman surprisingly encounters the articulated and cunning reptile – the serpent, Lucifer, and it induced her to eat of the Tree of the Knowledge of Good and Evil; and she in turn had Adam to do the same.

The immediate consequence of that act of disobedience was that they became aware of their nakedness. The question that needs to be asked at this juncture is what is nakedness? Were the animals, the monkeys, chimpanzees, and the donkeys naked? Is nakedness a state of mind? Prior to their act of disobedience, they saw each other in their nudity and were encouraged to explore each other's fascinating possibilities. Obviously, the other animals were exploring possibilities. In Chapter 1 verse 28, after he created them, God blessed them and said unto them, "be fruitful and multiply and replenish the earth...". In short, the Lord God told them to go and have sex. Obviously, they must have known to what other use their genitals could be put to. And later, and to the woman to reproduce: another aspect of the sexual connection.

And so again the question rises, what is meant by "...the eyes of them were both open and they knew that they were naked, and they tied fig leaves together and made themselves "aprons". Why aprons and not dresses? They both had breasts. The answer is simple. The apron covers the genitalia. In all of this, one sees the transposition of the Mosaic mindset in relation to the sexed thing as such; and more particularly in relation to the female gender.

Throughout Man's history, one discerns an unbalanced preoccupation with the "sexed thing". For that matter, it may be said that the central theme of man's morality is sex and the thrust of his achievement can directly or indirectly be related to that pelvic differential between man and woman. Virginity, where we make an issue of a tissue, has forever been linked with the "mother of God" – Virgin Mary. In the final verse of the Chapter it reads: "And they were both naked the man and his wife and were not ashamed". It is passing strange that the sacrament of Marriage was never alluded to by God in his creation mode.

The question that needs to be asked, what is peculiar about the "Knowledge" that makes nakedness something to be ashamed of? God created them naked and said go forth and multiply. From the very beginning they were aware that they were different and were further aware that this difference was specifically complimentary. So why the shame post the act of disobedience? A further question that needs to be asked is: "why is this knowledge so specific, so myopic? Is it because they only ate part of the fruit? Be that as it may, having eaten of the fruit what were the other consequences of that knowledge that reposed in that fruit? In what other way were they enlightened? That was never disclosed.

Consequent to their gastronomic experience, they were punished by God: even the serpent. We are of the opinion that the word " serpent" was used generically to describe the scaly, limbless reptile known as the serpent, the snake. Part of this punishment was that it would eat dust all the days of its life. We do, however, know that some are carnivorous and omnivorous. There is no dust pizza.

In relation to the woman, it is in part pain being inflicted on her during childbirth. God says: "I will greatly multiply thy sorrow and thy conception: in sorrow thou shall bring forth children." We discern no compassion, no forgiveness: only a vengeful God. And for what? In the legal corridors of our civilisation, there is a pronouncement that defines our concept of justice. The punishment must fit the crime. And God goes on to say that she shall have the "hots" only for her husband. Does that mean she was intended not to be promiscuous but should stand or lie only before Adam in her venereal passion? God, it seemed, frowned on promiscuity. And this body of punishment culminated in the denigrating statement that he Adam would rule over her. Subservience, servitude, inequality being celestially institutionalised.

Indeed, she would be his helper, his slave. All of this is predicated on the belief that when, in his punishing mode, God addresses himself not only to Adam and the woman Eve, but to generations of humankind. The ecclesiastical concept or tenet of "Original Sin" comes to mind. Where is the justice? With regard to Adam and his act of disobedience, his life would be one of perpetual strife and toil of an unforgiving earth until he died. It was at this time that Adam named the woman Eve. Having so punished them and it was an ongoing punishment until their terrestrial demise, he drove them out of the Garden of Eden. And his reason was this (Chapter 3-22): "Behold the man is become one of us, to know Good and Evil: and now lest he put forth his hand, and take also of the Tree of Life" and live forever...". Again a question that can be asked, is this: what is the nexus between "behold the man is become one of us" and human sexuality?

One very important question that comes to the fore is this: why were there two trees placed in the Garden of Eden? Assuming that Adam and Eve were endowed with free will, that would mean that they could choose, and once they had the power of choice, there was then the probability that they could choose to disobey. Having created two innocent beings, why place them in a situation of jeopardy? How many months and years could they have withstood that temptation? Is it logical to assume that Adam and Eve were born perfect? On their level as an image of God, could they have lived forever? The answer has to be in the negative since eternity for them reposed in the fruit of the Tree of Life. Therefore, they had to die or go through some sort of transformation as the decades went by. Or perhaps they could live eternally as human beings. That would have been the first and biblical oxymoron. But then, what about the process of growth and reproduction?

Adam and Eve quite evidently came into existence as adults (who could have breastfed them?) and in time would give birth to their children and who in time would also reproduce. A situation of incipient incest. And then a growth process leading to what?

At this time, we think it proper to explore what we choose to term as the phenomenon of Adam. And the exploration in its brevity is couched in two questions.

Was Adam perfect?

Was Adam immortal?

God created Adam out of the dust of the earth, breathed into his nostrils the breath of life, and he became a living soul. Assuming that this biblical narration pertaining to the provenance of Man / Adam, then Adam, when created and before his act of disobedience, could not experience the process of death since death was the punishment for his act of disobedience. Further, assuming that he did not disobey God, what would have been his terrestrial situation in relation to the notion of time? He could not have lived forever since he had not partaken of the Tree of Life (see Genesis 3-22). Since he could not have lived forever, what is the significance of the punishment of death? The situation is perplexing and somewhat irrational. But the only rational and logical question that can be asked is this: was death the punishment for this act of disobedience? A careful perusal of Genesis Chapters 3:17-18 would lead one to the ineluctable conclusion that death was not the punishment for the transgression by Adam and Eve. They each had their individual punishment, and death was the commonality of their collective terrestrial existence and destiny.

Adam was mortal. That place in Eden was to have been a paradise where living was to have been sheer enjoyment, and sex and procreation aspects of this joy and happiness. Through a descending order of incestuous sexual relations, the world would have been populated, and mankind would supposedly glorify his Creator forever. Would that be the raison d'être of mankind? His existential justification to be. What would have been his notion of joy, happiness, and satisfaction? Would all of this have been terrestrially grounded and finding sublime expression in human solidarity and togetherness?

With the effluxion of time, man would have acquired the knowledge that presently characterises modern man. Would he in time have explored the moon, the planets, and the stars? Man, homo sapiens, would have, but not from a stream of creation emanating from that place in Eden. Having been created from the dust of the earth and subject to death, was he again perfect? The answer is a categorical No. And so, the world and the community that he created could therefore not be perfect. So God directly and indirectly created an imperfect world. And so, the question that comes to the fore again and as previously mentioned, how can God, the quintessence of Perfection, create an imperfect world with its imperfect inhabitants? Is there a contradiction and divine impossibility? Simplistically, the answer is No.

Another aspect of this issue of perfection is that everything besides God was created and therefore subordinate to the perfection of God. The Earth, according to the biblical narrative, was created and from that, which was primarily created, Adam emerged, and therefore being twice removed from the source of creation. Hence it is not an impossibility and contradiction that which is the quintessence of perfection can create that which is less than perfect. On whatever level, it certainly would not make sense for God to create himself for in the process of self-creation he would be emasculating himself. He is God, he can do all things, he can create Good, he can create Evil, for he has no limitations. And the Good and Evil that we are contending with are divine constructs in a plan that we have not yet fully understood.

In reiteration, God can do all things. If he is unable to do Evil that would have been a limitation. For that matter it was God that introduced Evil in the Garden of Eden when there were two important trees: the Tree of Life and the Tree of Knowledge of Good and Evil. Adam was both mortal and imperfect and what was existentially consequential was that he had free-will: the power of choice. Without free-will there could be no evil as Evil is a critical aspect of the human condition. Man, therefore, can do Good and perpetrate Evil: and God knows that he is capable of both. He is Omniscient and he is Adam's Creator. Why create Man *qua* Adam when he knew that Adam will at sometime embark on a course of Evil?

By creating Man, God in his quintessential magnificence allowed himself to experience himself in a mode that transcends all other modes: and that is to experience himself as Love. Love is not static. It is dynamic in its ineffable multifarious epiphany. For example, it is caring, giving, loving, and forgiving. For that matter, forgiving could be perceived as the highest expression of love. He forgives our sins and by so doing enables man to attain the apotheosis of his humanity by forgiving his neighbour. And it is through the myriad acts of forgiveness that man approximates to the spiritual. For man, the reason to forgive is linked with the consequential pain that he experiences and that has been inflicted on him, so the act of forgiveness which is cathartic, sublimates his terrestrial proclivities.

Forgiveness as already indicated is an act of love or is love; and so by forgiving, the person who forgives and the person who is forgiven are inextricably bound in a new salubrious relationship. And so, it is love that forms the basis for our continued creative beneficence. It enables us to transcend our humanity and aligns us with the divine purpose of the Creator.

This alignment takes place in a world of time; and time can only be relevant and possible in a finite environment where the central characteristic is death. A man, therefore, could not be immortal as death was a condition precedent for his existence. If man were immortal, time would be of no relevance and of no significance. There would be no need, no urgency to progress. And if there was no need, no urgency, then Adam would have to be perfect. There would be nothing like human progress on, whatever the level in whatever the sphere.

In the final analysis, it is Death and Time that make human civilisation possible irrespective of its rise and fall. It is somewhat bizarre and paradoxical that instead of embracing Death and Finitude, we are petrified at the inevitable approach of Death. What Man should be doing is to celebrate Death and rejoice and revel in Life. Death and Life, they complement each other. Without either, Adam *qua* Man would not be here; and that is according to the Genesis narrative that defines the theory of Special Creation.

The sublime conundrum: God could not be God if he did not have the capacity to forgive the unrepentant. How can there, therefore, be a HELL?

IS WOMAN WOMAN BY VIRTUE OF A CERTAIN DISABILITY?

In antediluvian or Neanderthal times when Homo Sapiens (male) stood at the entrance of his cave facing the unknown and the dangers of the unknown, where was his female counterpart? Was she beside him, in front of him, or just behind him? In that arena of danger, she was conspicuously absent. She was in the innermost recesses of the cave suckling her young. He, the man, was in the arena of danger, providing for and protecting the family.

This existential posture was facilitated by his brutish strength and emerging cunning to meet the exigencies of his primordial circumstance. And the latter being a function of an evolving cerebral capacity. It is this evolving cerebral capacity that has given the man a certain cognitive superiority over his female counterpart at that time.

As he subdued his physical world, the experience engendered within him a certain confidence of self and, in relation to his female counterpart, a certain admiration for her man. And so on, one hand, there is confidence, the locus and provenance of which repose in the male. On the other hand, there is admiration: a female response to an objective male reality. In the ascendancy of human responses in an evolving world, the relational position of the male evinces a certain superiority vis-à-vis his female unfeathered biped.

The challenges of his evolving and primordial world trigger his cerebral component to an extent and degree that surpasses that of the female. And for her, the residual admiration with the effluxion of time provides her with a certain existential solace that defines her relationship with her male protector and innovator. She necessarily relies on him, but he, in turn, holds on to her in the context of a utilitarian necessity.

But with the passage of time, and the societal processes and challenges becoming more cerebral, the matrix of dependence that ensured her survival became less acute and necessary. A budding confidence of self and in-self began to emerge across the tumultuous legions of years. And so in the struggle of life for life on its various levels, she acquired knowledge, she acquired skills virtually on the same level as her male counterpart. And though she has excelled in the various spheres of human endeavour, the generality of her gender has in some measure been impeded by a certain stuttering disability.

From the entrance of his cave, Man resolutely marched into the unknown world: forever conquering, forever confident. And in the trail that he blazed, she and her offspring followed: forever admiring, forever pleasured, forever pleasurable.

And as they marched across the generations, and in relation to the female, the cave syndrome of dependence, subordination, and admiration virtually imprinted itself upon her psyche. And as regards her male counterpart, dominance and conquest defined his role and posture in the general scheme of things. The march was an evolutionary one, with Homo Sapiens becoming less animalistic, less brutish, and more rational. And so the two continued to evolve, conquering in their respective and various spheres the realms of thought and action that was made accessible by a critical metamorphosis of their cerebral faculty. But despite their leap across the generations of time, and during which the interpersonal relationship between man and woman assumed a very human face, the syndrome of the cave residually persisted.

Cooperation and partnership seem to characterise their relation in their secular and domestic world: but even then, there was a certain relational imbalance.

Regardless of how sophisticated their society, how erudite, the diminishing residue of the cave continues to manifest itself. Gender power was skewed in favour of the male in spite of female consciousness of its existence. Modern woman has been aware of this imbalance, which paradoxically is maintained by women in her collectivity, but tentatively reduced or minimised in her singularity.

Throughout the world of women, this phenomenon of gender imbalance or inequality is evident and will persist until the thrust of human evolution brings about a salubrious existential nexus between the genders. And this evolutionary thrust can only be actuated and consummated by women in their collectivity. It is only women who can liberate themselves from the syndrome of the cave.

It is not the role nor the responsibility of the male to assist her in her quest for transformational leadership.

He is not an impediment. At worst, he is an enabler by his disinterested posture; and it is left to her to make that leap into the circle of gender equilibrium. How can she be assisted if by being assisted the syndrome of the cave is given greater potency? She would be giving it life by assuming a posture of need across the gender divide.

She has all of what it takes to successfully make that leap – almost. The psyche is more or less wholesome, and the cerebral faculty attuned. The mundane capacities are almost in overdrive, and her heart is pulsating expectantly. Within her psyche, there is a struggle going on, and the outcome of which will characterologically define her in her sublime gender pulchritude and plenitude. There may be many evolutionary phases before the struggle ceases to be, but when it does, as it must, Gender Justice will have been attained. At this juncture, in her special evolution, Woman in her spiritual sublimity, her venereal pulchritude, her cerebral incandescence, and in her collectivity, lacks confidence in herself.

Look at the world around us: gender inequality is all so pervasive, all so ubiquitous regardless of the diverse ethnic and geographical expressions. From the time of the cave, she admired him, not herself. Did he admire her? Why? For the natural expression of a biological endowment! She admired him because of the recognition of a certain disability within herself. And a corollary to this awareness was a lack of confidence within herself. But as she evolved the capacity to do, to achieve became greater and greater, and on the template of her existence, female confidence began to emerge.

At this point in time (2016), there is still this residual Neanderthal admiration. And so, woman is still not fully liberated from herself. The "disability" in some measure is still there; and so the conversation among women must become more vociferous and ubiquitous.

This article, we hope, will engender a dialectical inquiry among the generality and collectivity of woman and in consequence thereof, expand the epistemic parameters of her ontology as it relates to the existential contradictions between her "being" and "becoming". There is a need for a reconciliation on the level of the psyche.

In reiteration, the struggle is hers, not his. She must embrace it and liberate herself as he, the male, smilingly awaits her deliverance. But when? Certainly not now. Our extant political situation evidences this unpreparedness, this inadequacy, this disability.

As I see it, the time (2014, 2015, 2016) was anything but fortuitous for the emergence of a virtually all-female political party to contest the recently consummated election exercise. The time was right, and this was evidenced by the alarming number of persons who did not vote. And flowing from this is the question, why didn't they vote? The answer, a critical level of frustration, dissatisfaction, and disappointment. Why didn't a virtually all-female party emerge in this morass of populist political negativity? The answer, a patent lack of confidence in WO-man.

And so, reverting to the titular question, is wo-man by virtue of a certain disability? The answer is blowing in the wind; but I can feel it. (QED)

I am not an anthropologist nor a formal student of Gender Relations. I am just a free thinker, as waves of thought carry me along the many streams of life.

CREATION: FROM GOD[3] TO MAN

Did the UNCAUSED CAUSE (UC) create Man - Homo Sapiens? If so, why? Man evolved, and like all other sentient beings he is not a direct creation of the UNCAUSED CAUSE, but a manifestation of the eternal magnificence of the UC, and which is evidenced in the universe of "becoming".

Before going further, one must be able to differentiate the metaphysical difference between "being" and "becoming". Those who subscribe to the notion, the theory of creation, unavoidably predicate their position on the Bible; and in particular the chapter of Genesis. The totality of Christianity is anchored to the Genesis narrative. And according to that narrative, all sentient beings, the plants, the birds, the fishes and the animals (flora and fauna) were created by the UNCAUSED CAUSE : GOD.

For me, and particularly in relation to the creation of Man, I find his biblical mode of coming into existence contradictory, simplistic, terrestrial and problematic. For Homo Sapiens there were two distinct modes of creation. One in relation to the male, Adam, the other in relation to the female, Eve.

---

[3] The word God is generic and it encompasses the appellations, the Uncaused Cause, the First Principle, Jesus, Jehovah, Allah and so forth. My preference is the UNCAUSED CAUSE.

According to Genesis 1:26, Man is created out of nothingness, but out of the image and likeness of the UNCAUSED CAUSE (UC). What is that image, what is that likeness since the UC has no form. To have form he must have boundaries and the UNCAUSED CAUSE has no boundaries since he is the repository of all boundaries. Thus, the form of Homo Sapiens is one of its many and eternal forms. As I see it that mode of creation befits the UC.

But then in Genesis 2:7 it reads:

And the Lord God formed Man of the dust of the ground and breathed into his nostrils the breath of life and Man Became a living Soul.

But what he created was male. The question I now ask is, why male, why not female? Already I can perceive the institutionalisation of discrimination between the sexes. Having created Man, the male thing, the UNCAUSED CAUSE assumed the role of a planter; and subsequent thereto it became aware of the solitude of that male thing, "Man", and felt that he should have a companion.

At this juncture the second act of creation comes to the fore. And in Genesis 2:21& 22 it reads:

And the Lord God caused a deep sleep to fall upon Adam and he slept; and he took one of his ribs and closed upon the flesh instead thereof and the rib which the Lord had taken from the man, made he a woman and brought her unto Adam.

In this scenario we have the first organ transplant and use of anaesthesia in a medical context on earth.

The question I now ask myself is, why this mechanical, mundane and pedestrian mode of creation when It could have thought, wished or willed Adam and Eve into existence. The answer very simply is this. It is ordinary men, thinking like ordinary men in conformity with their
ordinary knowledge and experience, that could allude to this mode of creation.

Why would the UNCAUSED CAUSE breathe into a pair of nostrils to create a living entity? Why would the UC perform complex surgery to bring into existence Homo Sapiens? As I see it, the theory of Special Creation is to crassly simplistic to reflect the magnificent grandeur of the UNCAUSED CAUSE. The theory/ reality of evolution does since it creates the logical possibility for there to be other sentient beings in the universe.

As I see it, among the stars, the planets and the galaxies, Homo Sapiens are not alone. His cousins in whatever their form are there; for evolution, unlike creation, is not static, it is intrinsically dynamic. It is in conformity with the UNCAUSED CAUSE with its limitless possibilities.

In very recent times the fossil of Homo X was found and was determined to have been in existence about 300,000 years ago (carbon dating). IT was not Homo Sapiens but Homo X. Evolution comes to mind.

The biblical narrative for some of its parts is like a story, a fable. Some of its constituent parts and allusions can be found in ancient texts that pre-date the bible, and the Bible has been around for about 3,400 years. Compared to those ancient texts, it is an adolescent. These ancient religious and cultural texts go back as far as 36,000 years BC. For example: (1) The Emerald tablets - 36,000 BC; (2) The Sumerian Texts - 2,500 BC; (3) The Hammurabi Code - 2,500BC; (4) The Atrahassis text - 1650 BC; (5) the Wisdom of Amenemope Text - 1075 BC; (6) The Dead Sea Scrolls - 250 BC; (7) The Septuagint Old Testament - 132 BC.

It is to be noted that most of the biblical narratives can be found in many ancient cultures and texts that pre-date the Bible. And so, the question that comes to the fore is this: is the biblical version of creation a divinely inspired narrative or a plagiarised event from the cultures and religions of the very ancient past? I vote for the latter.

As I see it, the UNCAUSED CAUSE in the exercise of its boundless love and magnificence threw into the ether the seed of life that contained divers possibilities for evolving. It was not a mindless, purposeless, evolutionary process that was envisaged, but a sharing in the divine magnificence of the UC. That sharing is called LOVE; and it is LOVE that makes all things possible. From the rising of the sun, the explosion of the galaxies, the birth of humans and the death of all sentient beings. The UC guides the evolutionary process towards its Omega point when all will be subsumed in the numinous magnificence of the UNCAUSED CAUSE.

So Homo Sapiens, that is Modern Man, has evolved along a chain of organic events; in some measure from theCatarrhines (the apes) – 25 million years ago, to the chimpanzees 8 to 6 million years ago, to Homo Erectus, now extinct, and now to Homo Sapiens, the Modern Man. It has been a progressive process characterised at this point in time by the emergence of a reasoning faculty. Homo Sapiens is now moral and rational and with a conscience. Accountability and responsibility are now his lot: a condition of being that has now prepared him for the next evolutionary level.

He has now evolved to the DIGITAL AGE and from there ineluctably to the ROBOTIC AGE and which will be followed by the AGE OF LEISURE. From this platform he will emerge unto the SPIRITUAL AGE where he will have metamorphosed into HOMO SPIRITUS; thus being more spiritual than human.

THE OMNICOSMIC⁴ RAMBLINGS

I t has been perceived that the Past cannot be lived, just as the Future cannot be lived: the former as sometimes perceived is a dream, ethereal of some consequence, of some significance but unalterable. Realistically speaking, it is eternal stasis that cannot be duplicated or reified in the inexorable movement of time. However, it is vital, for without the rainbow of human living it would not be possible and the values that define Homo Sapiens could not subsist in a world without a Past. Thus, the immaterial informs the material and the tapestry of human existence obtains its evolutionary vitality.

The Past is dead: but the Past is alive. It is this contradiction that provided hope for all mankind in its diverse eschatological aspirations. If there is a Past there must be a Present; and if there is a Past and a Present there must be a Future. Has the Present any limit? If the Present or the "now" were to stop at this point in time, what happens? What is next? Does the cessation of thePresent mean the cessation of Time, the extinction of Man? Is the notion of the Present, the notion of Time, a figment of the imagination or just a construct of the Mind? More comprehensively, is the notion of the Present, of Time, of Homo Sapiens the figment of "something's" imagination: a figment of an Omnicosmic Mind? Is there a

---

4 The "Omnicos" is a word coined by me. It means all that is within and beyond the Cosmos. Is it the FIRST PRINCIPLE

transcendental nexus between all of this and the consciousness of a supernatural entity – the Uncaused Cause? Intriguing questions.

But then, is there a dualism between that Consciousness and that Principle? Or are they one and the same and evidencing an omnicosmic unity? But then, that unity is not static. In its eternal magnificence it unfolds, and thus bringing into existence the notion of Time. And thereby making possible the epiphany of sentient beings in their structural, emotional, cognitive and intellectual diversity. The latter three being an epiphenomenon of the physical structural matrix: in particular the Brain.

All sentient beings possess a brain, however defined, and the fundamental commonality of its non-physical function is awareness. But this faculty of awareness varies in its intensity and sophistication that is, in functional alignment with its intrinsic etiology. Hence Homo Sapiens, which is the apotheosis of terrestrial creation, has the patent capacity to explore and engage with the physical and metaphysical dimensions of his world/being. And it is this capacity that of necessity makes for him, Time, a categorical existential imperative. The composite of Time is the Past, the Present/Now and the Future; and what is remarkable and unique about the Past and the Future is that they both influence the "now". What is further remarkable about the Future is that it does not exist. Past and Future both utilitarian in relation to the Present. Therein lies the paradox of human existence. From an ontological perspective, the Future is Being and Becoming: it is and it is not and thus it encompasses and transcends the gamut of human existence.

Thus the phenomenon of the Future portends the "Being" not the existence of the Uncaused Cause and for which the three categories, the Past, the Present and the Future are of no consequence. Omniscience, Omnipotence and Omnifience are constitutive elements of the Uncaused Cause, but not from a pluralistic and definitional perspective; and for which the Now is eternal. Though Homo Sapiens partake of the Now, it is not sublimely and quintessentially of the Now: and it is this fact that ushers in his inevitable mortality – his inexorable embrace of Death. All sentient beings in their own mode and time must die. Homo Sapiens must effect this terrestrial demise for the very simple reason that he is time bound. So what is Death? Is it the absolute cessation of physical activity and which encompasses cerebral activity? Sine the brain is itself physical/material the constructs of awareness, cognition and emotion therefore cease. However, the Uncaused Cause is all creating, an activity *qua* "Being" that has no end, and hence this cessation that we speak of is a transition into another form, mode and level of "Becoming". It is a process that continues until at some critical juncture is subsumed into the First Principle or the Uncaused Cause. The process enables the First Principle to enjoy its limitless, ineffable, multifarious and absolute magnificence. This enjoyment embraces Homo Sapiens in its totality: and this embrace is unreserved Love. What embraces and what is embraced are inextricably entwined, since Love by its transcendental quiddity abhors division, divisiveness, alienation and estrangement.

Homo Sapiens is an aspect of this process of creation. In its specificity it is a project with its own immanent aetiology that binds it to that which is intrinsically eternal. As a project, its processes of living are not by mere chance but are guided and determined by a supreme intelligence, which in a very abstruse manner ensures its ultimate consummation within the embrace of the Divine. What pellucidly must be understood is that Homo Sapiens in its material existence is the function of the Past, the Present and the Future. Without one or the other he ceases to be human though he does not cease to exist. On whatever level or mode he is evolving towards an Omega point: towards a higher level of spirituality.

At this juncture certain questions come to mind. What is the nexus between Homo Sapiens' materiality and eternal spirituality? Where do the issues of Good and Evil, Free-Will and Accountability fit into all of this? As has already been intimated, creation is predicated upon the quintessential magnificence of the Uncaused Cause, which going beyond the limits of all that is human, is Spiritual. And it is this reality of "Being" that futuristically imports a necessary paradoxical dualism in the becoming and being of Homo Sapiens. Man therefore is both material and spiritual; and it is there that one sees the inexplicable convergence of the Now and the Future, which in the matrix of the eternal are one and the same.

Everyone has the power of Choice. No one can escape the necessity of Choice; and so the life of Homo Sapiens is a composite of choices. He is not an automation since Choice and Rationality, whatever their level of manifestation, are *a priori* consequent to each other: but the latter facilitates the other. The necessity of Choice gives rise to the notion of Morality, and Morality is peculiar only to the affairs of Homo Sapiens. And it is only in relation to his conduct that this notion of Morality can be ascribed. Morality therefore is an epiphenomenon of human conduct and defines the value system of Homo Sapiens. It has certain specificity but yet it is universal. It is this existential dualism that brings to the fore, and on a terrestrial plane, the notion of Good and Evil in its mundane relativity: and which is a function of Man's geography and his historical and cultural circumstance. Evil is a function of Choice. Good is a function of Choice. And both are inextricably entwined in the circumstance of humanity.

The Good is that which is in conformity with the morality of Homo Sapiens, his particularity and universality. Evil is a departure therefrom. From a metaphysical perspective, Good "is" and Evil "is not". The sublime and eternal magnificence of the Uncaused Cause is incompatible with the existence of Evil. What needs to be understood is that there are different dimensions of existence in relation to sentient beings; and with regard to the Uncaused Cause there is only Magnificence and Transcendence in their absolute manifestation and Unity. The "one" is, and all is subsumed in the "One": for it is the Uncaused Cause, the First Principle, God, Jehovah that is the "One". The Creator of the Universe, the Creator of the Cosmos, the Creator of Homo Sapiens. He is Quintessential, Eternal, Absolute and Magnificent. And Man is a pale reflection of Himself: and hence in the "image of GOD he created them".

BEING AND BECOMING

When one considers the majestic expanse of the Universe with its constituent elements of galaxies, planets, stars and asteroids beyond measure, the ineluctable and logical conclusion that can be arrived at is that the Universe by its cosmic symmetry did not come about by mere chance. It had to have a Beginning and therefore must have an End. And it is this juxtapositioning of what is the Beginning and the End that introduces the construct of Time and hence making possible the emergence of sentient beings. For without Time, sentient beings including man would not exist as it is this epiphenomenon of Time that makes possible the materiality of Becoming.

Antecedent to the Beginning is BEING, which is the First Principle or the UNCAUSED CAUSE. And not being caused has no constraints, no limitations and therefore is beyond Time. That which is within Time is "Becoming" and therefore subject to the principle of evolution which is a function of Time.

Man is a sentient being and therefore is constrained by Time. He has a beginning and he has an end. His very ontology dictates that. But when he effects his temporal and terrestrial demise his Beginning and his End is subsumed into what is no longer "Becoming". He no longer exists for to exist is Time. He is of

BEING and of the UNCAUSED CAUSE. He is immortal and supernatural. Death therefore is indeed the Gateway to this state of being. And the question that arises, is there a consequential nexus to this transition?

It is to be noted then that Man is a sentient being with Free-Will that imports rationality; and in all probability did exercise that Will untowardly. He is not perfect. And it is the exercise of that Will that introduced into his sentient world the construct of JUSTICE with its immanent notion of Good and Evil. The two characterise the rational world of "Becoming"; and in relation to the UNCAUSED CAUSE, it is a sub principle that is and is not. That sub principle permeates the world of the rationally sentient being and hence thus making Good and Evil the central ambiguity of the human condition. They are subservient to the FIRST PRINCIPLE and their existence is contingent on the factor of Time and on the notion, the construct of "Becoming".

But then Good and Evil are not opposite. They are apposite: apt in the circumstance of humanity and are teleologically linked to the FIRST PRINCIPLE since they are of the FIRST PRINCIPLE, the UNCAUSED CAUSE. And it is this that gives rise to the conundrum of the genesis of Good and Evil. They are separate and apart and, in the realm of human affairs, are personified in the beings of Jesus, Allah, Jehovah, Lucifer, Satan the Devil.

Individually, they are not BEING: the UNCAUSED CAUSE. But they do have a role to play in the numinous drama of the eternally unfolding FIRST PRINCIPLE. And it is this thespian posture on its diverse plane of "Becoming" that makes it possible for the Good to evolve into the best version of itself.

Whereas the evolution of the Good is exponential and hence its inevitable communion with the eternally unfolding, Evil on the other hand is eternally regressive to its end. It is not BEING nor "Becoming". Its existence is residual but purposive. It is bound by time until it regresses into the unadulterated quintessence of nihilism. Until such time, the dynamics of contending forces facilitate the continuous and progressive emergence of numinous attributes that conflate with the quiddity, the essence of BEING. These attributes are Love, Justice, Compassion and Reason. Their absence would result in a cosmic void in the universal plan of BEING. Homo Sapiens would not exist. For in the very matrix of BEING it is these primary elements that has occasioned the emergence of Man as the culmination of "Becoming" with its spiritual possibilities and potentialities.

Man is a composite: he is both Good and Evil: he is of BEING but not "Becoming": he is BEING in potency and hence in conformity and congruous with "Perfection". Futility is not an aspect of BEING, hence Homo Sapiens though he has an existential end serves a divine purpose for the UNCAUSED CAUSE. And it is a cause that glorifies his MAKER, his Creator, BEING, the UNCAUSED CAUSE, the FIRST PRINCIPLE. And Evil, which has regressed into "Nothingness", is that which is NOT.

A PAROXYSM OF BEWILDERMENT

Indeed I was overwhelmed by a paroxysm of bewilderment when I heard these three utterances by the Honourable Prime Minister (at the time). They were:

1.   We (Homo Sapiens) have to **co-exist** with **Covid-19**.

2.   **Colonialism** has a **Conscience**.

3.   The **TRUTH** is what you believe the truth to be.

With regard to the first, what did he mean in its exactitude or inexactitude? The public response did not reverberate along the corridors of my mind. There seem to be a general acceptance as to its relevance and rectitude which left me somewhat perplexed.

As regards the second and third, his surrogates endeavoured to explain away or imbue them with some dubious meaning of no consequence in order to protect him from himself.

The First Utterance.

We (Homo Sapiens) have to co-exist with Covid-19.

In the first instance of disbelief, no one attempted to intervene or placate my linguistic sensibilities; or is it because I was wrong in the posture that I had assumed in relation to the content, context, grammatical meaning and implication of the statement made? Was it a valid statement to be reassuringly embraced by a community in its pandemic mitigation endeavour?

How can one co-exist with an implacable enemy whose existential justification is to effectuate one's terrestrial demise once an opportunity presents itself? The march of the virus is inexorable towards human annihilation. It has no **conscience**, no sensitivity, no human element that could create a relational template for engagement.

Covid-19 has no soul, no heart, no empathy, no compassion, no remorse, no discerning comparative faculty and no value system. As far as I am concerned, **Covid-19** is **Death**. On what level is it possible to co-exist with death? To co-exist implies a functional harmony in spite of differences in interest, ideology, *modus operandi* and *modus vivendi*. Is it possible for homo sapiens to establish a relationship when death denies a relationship, precludes a relationship and is anathema to relationships?

We may have to co-exist with the protocols, the vaccines that are coming into existence to deny the existence of Covid-19. Coexistence promotes the continuance of different state of affairs or being that in their diverse essence, aims and objectives are functionally and existentially compatible on some minimal but sustainable level. And so, whatever the level, Covid-19 is not compatible with Homo Sapiens.

The Second Utterance.

Colonialism has a Conscience.

The second perplexing utterance is that **Colonialism has a Conscience**. As I see it, colonialism is a pseudo refined extension of slavery. And that is from the perspective of the colonised masses. It is a geopolitical policy where one or more countries acquires full or partial control over another country, occupying it with settlers and exploiting its human and natural resources. The control has a certain quasi legitimacy since the colonised state acquiesces to the control under a dubious and questionable acceptance of its beneficial role in the exchange of goods, services and benefits. But the pernicious aspect of this type of governance is that the colonial policy is geared towards the ultimate utilisation of that which is best for the coloniser; its own aggrandisement. The benefits to the colonised is at best functionally incidental and collateral.

This system or policy of colonialism has no conscience since its raison d'etre is predicated on greed and malevolent acquisition that is tempered with a spurious, superficial and contrived benevolence. There is no conscience, just crass and opportunistic acquisition that is diabolically and calculatingly measured to gain a level of acceptance and tolerance by the colonised state. Thus the colonised masses experience a veneer of social and economic justice under an imported system that simulates the rule of Law.

Before the Prime Minister made his political declaration to that which he perceived as the profane herd, he should with due circumspect, have assessed the intellectual depth of his supporters and others, since some of them despite their patent sycophancy are quite astute and knowing. Incidentally, party hacks can be "degreed" individuals. But then a PhD in whatever area of human endeavour does not preclude stupidity and asininity in other areas of life including politics writ large.

So Colonialism has a Conscience is the quintessence of stupidity.

And when a Minister of Government in a disappointing endeavour to explain away and to save the then Prime Minister from himself, I would like to remind her that there were human beings who conceptualised, managed and operationalised the death camps at **AUSCHWITZ**.

What must pellucidly be understood or made patently clear is that **Conscience** is a function of our morality and it is the trigger that alerts our sensibilities as to the rectitude of human behaviour. It is a portal that opens up unto the spiritual and defines our relationship with our fellow homo sapiens. It puts a certain value of consequence on our interactions with each other in a manner and to a degree that, the implications and intimations of our individual conduct are in conformity with expectations that transcend ourselves. And it is this transcendence that aligns itself with the spiritual composition of our being. And thus, its attempted association with Colonialism is a spurious and macabre juxtaposition that gives rise to that which is irrelevant and devoid of meaning.

COLONIALISM is a construct emanating from man's greed, whereas CONSCIENCE is an abstraction that reposes in the hearts and souls of Man. Finally and most importantly RACISM is inherent in Colonialism.

The Third Utterance.

The Truth is what you believe the truth to be.

If that is indeed so, then there is no truth since what is truth would have become an individualised universal commodity. Truth would have become relative and subjective, and the constancy of truth, and that is what makes it "truth", would have become a figment of an illusionary imagination.

An opinion can be individualised, though it can be shared, accepted and internalised. Truth from a metaphysical perspective "is". Being is its essence whereas "becoming" characterises that which can be categorised as opinion. The truth is not the function of one's belief since one's belief system can be made up of a plethora of opinionated elements that do not conform to empirical reality. The truth can be your belief but your belief does not fall into the category of truth. I believe that the earth is round and there are those who believe that the world is flat. Contextually, my belief conforms to truth; but for the other his belief and the truth are world's apart.

If your Truth is what you believe the truth to be, how can I have faith and place reliance on that which is individualised, subjective and goes contrary to an empirical reality? Truth is "being" and opinion is "becoming". Therein lies the metaphysical divide.

BRYAN'S TRIBUTE

I t is with the most profound sadness and regret that I have assumed this responsibility of reading out to you this short tribute on behalf of my Friend, **BRYAN RUFUS EDWARD WALCOTT**: affectionately called by me BRY. Had I known that his formal and nascent designation was Bryan Rufus Edward Walcott we would at the Vigie beach baptised him **BREW**. That, however, did not come to pass; and so for me he was BRY, my friend.

This is a rather short tribute to a man I got to know at virtually the very sunset of his years. He was a wonderful human being: brilliant in many ways and on many levels. He was a gentleman par excellence and he was my friend.

He was not my contemporary when I think of his tenure at St. Mary's College, his youthful working life and his early life as a husband and father. There are those who can speak most authoritatively of those times; friends like Emsco, Brani, Kernan, Mauri, Archie, Rollo and others. I was not so fortunate. Though I saw him around the city then, I knew of him for many years. But by the end of his life he became my friend and I loved him like a brother. It took Brani, Kernan, Rollo, Archie, Mauri and the others a lifetime to love him. But between us our love transcended both space and time.

Comparatively and contextually speaking, our association crystallised or metamorphosed into a profound all encompassing friendship that extended beyond the mundane, the terrestrial, the secular; and epitomised a friendship that was quintessentially fulfilling. Indeed, I must say that there are few persons whose acquaintance is beyond price; and he my friend, Bry, unequivocally fell into that category.

Though our cosmology and eschatology differed, we shared a certain spirituality that made possible or facilitated that sublime and hilarious friendship. There were times when we were very serious and profound in our many discourses. But there were times when laughter elevated and sublimated our mundane exchanges as they relate to the foibles of human interaction, experiences, doings and undoings.

By now, you will have noticed that I have used the term friend or friendship a multiplicity of times; and for very good reason. For, in my opinion, friendship between two men transcends the heterosexual since the absence of the biological difference purifies the matrix of interaction, sublimates feelings of complementarity and brings into fruition the ideal unity of being.

And so, in the words of Kahlil Gibran, let me tell you of the friendship that Bry and myself shared:

"And a youth said, Speak to us of Friendship.

And he answered, saying:

Your friend is your needs answered.

He is your field which you sow with love and reap with thanksgiving.

And he is your board and your fireside.

For you come to him with your hunger

And you seek him for peace.

When your friend speaks his mind you fear not the "nay" in your own mind, nor do withhold the "ay".

And when he is silent your heart ceases not to listen to his heart;

For without words, in friendship all thoughts, all desires, all expectations are born and shared, with joy that is unclaimed.

When you part from your friend, you grieve not:

For that which you love most in him may be clearer in his absence, as the mountain to the climber is clearer from the plain.

And let there be no purpose in friendship save the deepening of the spirit.

For love that seeks aught but the disclosure of its own mystery is not love but a net cast forth: and only the unprofitable is caught.

And let your best be for your friend.

If he must know the ebb of your tide, let him know its flood also.

For what is your friend that you should seek him with hours to kill?

Seek him always with hours to live.

For it is his to fill your need, but not your emptiness.

And in the sweetness of friendship let there be laughter, and sharing of pleasures.

For in the dew of little things the heart finds its morning and is refreshed."

~ The Prophet

At this juncture it would be remiss of me not to indulge you in our five years of afternoons that we spent at the southern end of the Vigie Beach. I would arrive at 4.00pm and he would arrive at 5.00pm, after I had had my one mile walk. We then made our way to the sea. He would walk up to his knees and then dive and swim southward; since my cold threshold was lower than his, I would walk up to my neck and then follow. Having swam for about 100 yards we would stop and there the talks, the arguments, the debates and the discourses began. A most edifying period of time.

Sometimes we were joined by the regulars and irregulars. Brani fell between the regular and irregular, and his comings, not his goings, were unpredictable. We would converse for the better part of an hour and then make our way to the shore.

Depending on the occasion, we would imbibe. A libation to Bachuus, Themis, Athena, Neptune or Zeus depending on our frame of mind; and thus bring down the curtain of night on our marine excursion. We would then leave for our respective abodes; he to the North and I to the South.

At the close of our years we spoke about Death and Dying. These talks were never morbid nor depressing. From an abstruse perspective could even be scintillating.

Death and dying: this brings to mind the Prophet.

For what is it to die but to stand naked in the wind and to melt in the sun?

And what is it to cease breathing, but free the breath from its restless tides that it may rise and expand and seek GOD unencumbered.

Only when you drink from the river of silence shall you indeed sing. And when you have reached the mountain top, then you shall begin to climb. And when the earth shall claim your limbs, then shall you truly dance.

As I effect my departure from this ecclesiastical edifice I shall make my way to the site of my friend's internment, and from there I shall resolutely go the Vigie Beach to have a last swim with and for my friend. And there in the presence of his absence and in consonance with my eschatology I shall tell my friend this:

That in a little while, a moment of rest upon the wind and another woman shall bear him.

Farewell Bry.

Fare thee well my friend.

SECTION 361: CAPITULATION OR ENLIGHTENMENT

Y ear after year we have heard allusions with regard to Section 361 of the Criminal Code 2001, which no longer forms part of our criminal jurisprudence. Greater minds than ours in their constitutional exuberance perceived an aberration that deleteriously struck at the heart of at least one of our constitutional Freedoms: the Freedom of Expression. It is a perception which we have had difficulty to embrace on a legal and commonsensical level.

This Section which was titled "Spreading False News" (and that is instructive) reads thus:

"Everyone who wilfully publishes a statement, tale or news that he or she knows is false and that causes or is likely injury or mischief to a public interest, is guilty of an indictable offence and is liable to imprisonment for a term not exceeding two years."

This section was repealed by an amendment to the Criminal Code (No.38/2006).

The Sector that specifically took umbrage to this piece of legislation was the media: the Fourth Estate. It held the opinion that one of our constitutionally enshrined Fundamental Rights and Freedoms was being subverted and compromised as this Right embraced the Protection of our Freedom of Expression.

The question that comes to the fore is this: in what way is that fundamental right/freedom being infringed or undermined? In what way Section 361 poses a danger to the society and emasculates the Media's vaunted rights of expression?

To answer this question, the legalistic mode must be reduced to the pedestrian, plebeian the mundane on a somewhat graphic template. If we were to read this section on the Ciceron Mini bus the commuters therein. would in no way feel threatened. But the Grave Yard youth. with a certain criminal propensity and intent. would. For the rest of us the Lucian concept of freedom. would be abundantly manifest and protected in its. pristine ubiquitous and functional pulchritude.

If a wayward and misguided journalist were to at this time to publish in his media organ that Saint Lucia is afflicted with an epidemic of Saars or Mad Cow disease the consequence would impact most inimically on at least the Public Sector of Tourism. Tourist arrival would be reduced drastically and our economic viability would be severely crippled. It is common knowledge that we do not have an epidemic of Saars or Mad Cow disease in Saint Lucia at this time. With this fatuous repeal of Section 361, our rogue journalist, would with impunity, be laughing at his very sick joke. And our enlightened constitutionalists wallowing in a miasma of hubris.

The raison d'être of every piece of legislation, that is contextually speaking, is predicated on a societal prophylactic principle. What is the mischief that is intended to be averted? And in this regard we shall allude to Chapter 1, section 10 of the Saint Lucia Constitution Order 1978. It reads:

Except with his own consent, a person shall not be hindered in the enjoyment of his freedom of expression, including:

- *freedom to hold opinions without interference*
- *freedom to receive ideas and information without interference*
- *freedom to communicate ideas and information without interference (whether the communication be to the public generally or to any person or class of persons); and*
- *freedom from interference with his correspondence.*

1. *Nothing contained in or done under the authority of any law shall be held to be inconsistent with or in contravention of this section to the extent that the law in question makes provision –*

   (a) That is reasonably required in the interest of defence, public order, public morality or public health.

(b) and (c) and that imposes so far as that provision or as the case may be, the thing done under the authority thereof is shown not to be reasonably justifiable in a democratic society.

A rather succinct explication of the section is that a person shall not be hindered in the enjoyment of his or her freedom of expression. It is to be noted that most Media houses are corporate entities and as such are legal persons. As we all know, a corollary of freedom is responsibility and that responsibility is defined and expressed by what reasonably and imperatively obtains within a democratic society. And the constitutive elements of a democratic society in some measure are defence/security, public order, public safety, public morality and public health.

The subversion of any of these would pose a serious threat to the survival and continuance of our civilisation.And so, the question that now arises is what is the nexus between this constitutional right and **Section 361**? As we, for the greater part envisage it, this section deals with the regulation of the press; not from the point of view of private wrongs or civil injuries but from the view point of a public wrong or crime. A public wrong of the community in its social aggregate capacity.

Section 361 was neither ultra vires the Executive and Legislative Branches of Government. nor was it an infringement of Section 10 of the Constitution. On the contrary it was in sublime functional conformity with it and in no way derogated from the duties and rights subsumed under the principle of Freedom of is not constitutionally odious. And in this regard, one needs to address one's mind to certain words and phrases that establish the rectitude, legitimacy, functionality and validity of that section. And they are, "wrongfully", "knows is false", "causes injury", "mischief", and a "public interest".

However perceived or interpreted, this section is bereft of any meaning that would be deleterious to the norms that obtain in a democratic society. It is protective of society and its system members and sublimates the quality of life aspired therein. Its criminological rectitude is beyond repute since the elements of mens rea and actus reus are evidentially and linguistically conspicuous. And most importantly, it pronounces on a mischief that must be avoided and denounced in a civilised community of men/women.

Why was Section 361 repealed? The answer eludes our "free thinking" mind as it further indulges in its jurisprudential and philosophical ruminations.

Was the Leader of a Party coerced or seduced?

CARNIVAL AND ITS EMBRACE OF NAKEDNESS

To the Biblical Adherents:

When God created Adam and Eve, they for some time pranced around the Garden of Eden (perhaps for some months or years) in their pristine nakedness. Then at a critical juncture, and without producing any progeny, they partook of the fruits of the tree of Knowledge of Good and Evil. Also created was the tree of Life and of which we know very little about; why and why was it created?

And so we had Adam and Eve, very well endowed sexually and otherwise, enjoying the fruits and animals of that garden. Being fully endowed did they indulge in sexual activities? Were they aware of what uses their sex organs could be put to? If not, why not? They were not created as infants but as fully grown adults without disabilities, and that could take and understand instructions from their God. And since they were created fully endowed, human activities were quite natural to them. In a very natural environment they behaved naturally in their nakedness, and were not ashamed.

As regards the tree of Knowledge of Good and Evil, the directive given by God was only to Adam since Eve hay yet to be created. And this directive was as follows:

"Of every tree of the Garden of Eden thou mayest freely eat; but of the Tree of Knowledge of Good and Evil thou shall not eat; for in the day thou eatest thereof thou shall surely die."

Did Adam know what dying entailed; what were the consequences of death? It was subsequent to that divine directive that Eve was created. What if Adam had partaken of that fruit before the terrestrial emergence of Eve? But then, God knowing all things, past, present and the future, could not permit such cosmic and ecclesiastical confusion. Eve obviously must have been told of that directive by Adam and her motivation to disobey was not lascivious in terms of her hopes, expectations and propensities. She wanted to be wise; she wanted to be knowledgeable: she wanted to be like God. What was her sin? Murder, Grand Theft, Indecent Assault, Rape? As I see it, her sin was inspissated arrogance and or Hubris. For Adam, it was Disobedience to his God, Grievous gullibility and Hubris. Indiscretions of the Mind for both of them nothing; in the realm of things venereal. So why the allusion to shame and nakedness?

When they were created they were without clothes. They saw each other without clothes. Should there really be a difference at this time between seeing each other with clothes and without clothes? In a very natural world they behaved quite naturally in their nakedness and were not ashamed at their nakedness. Does that mindset import a peculiar and grotesque behavioural posture? Were they to be ashamed of his penis and or vulva? What about their breasts and their bum-bum?

What has to be kept in mind is the Tree of Knowledge of Good and Evil; two fundamental categories of "Becoming". Two existential templates that define mankind and its circumstance. Eve was not ashamed of her femaleness, nor Adam his maleness. It was there for all of Eden to see. For a whole "year" they feasted their eyes on their individual nakedness: then on the morning post their "gastronomic experience" they were ashamed. Nothing has changed except their state of mind, their body of knowledge: not in terms of their "genderness" but in terms of their all encompassing ontology. They saw in themselves the Good, the Evil: they perceived goodness and bad: the pure and the depraved; and they were ashamed.

They were ashamed. They were not hiding their ontological nakedness which could not be kept hidden physically but symbolically. And that was the role of the "fig leaf". They were hiding the totality of themselves from the "Great Betrayal". And so, from the very beginning nakedness was not something evil, something bad, something to be ashamed, something to be abhorred. In many a civilisation, man and women conducted their daily living in varying states of undress and which could be attributed to the exigencies of climate, hygiene and personal and societal conveniences.

In the Garden of Eden with God around, nakedness was the norm. There was no nexus between depravity and spirituality. But after the **"fall"** which had nothing to do with nakedness, a certain awareness, consciousness and reality emerged that fundamentally and existentially transformed the *modus operandi* and *modus vivendi* of both Adam and Eve. And that transformation had nothing to do with what was essentially sexual.

In Genesis, the God said, **"be fruitful and multiply"** that is after he had created the birds and animals. After he created Adam and Eve that was not said to them. Wouldn't it would have been superfluous seeing the Man was cerebral. Are we to assume that in an environment of rabid sexuality, the dogs, the rabbits, the donkeys, the gorillas, the chimpanzees, Adam and Eve did not make the logical and biological connection considering their complementary endowments? When Adam had an erection? Is it only the **"gastronomic fall"** or event that Adam became aware of the complementary orifice of Eve? And there were two.

The point that is being made is that there is no consequential nexus between nakedness and spirituality. As Man multiplied and evolved from foragers to settlements, taboos, rules, regulations and laws progressively circumscribed their *modus vivendi*. And some of these taboos and laws strictly controlled their interaction and relationships with each other. But nakedness was never a situation of wild abandonment that bordered to vulgarity. As the various tribal civilisations evolved, various aspects of community living became absorbed into religious activities with controlled nakedness forming part of diverse civil and religious festivities.

VOILA la Carnival!!! A secular activity in a somewhat spiritual/religious context. It is now 2024 with thousands of years of evolution. At this point we have gone beyond the **Great Wall of China**, which was creative and utilitarian. And now, in the context of our Carnival, we have the Bum-Bum Wall which is certainly not creative and utilitarian but expositional. Have we in some measure regressed? Fifty years ago there was partial nakedness in our Carnival and with the female cohort more partial than her male counterpart. Why more? But that is another story.

It is to be noted that the **Bum-Bum Wall** is female in composition and in our present context of societal sophistication and discrimination we now associate alarming degrees of undress or nakedness with the females. It is to be further noted that the **Wall** is tainted by an element of vulgarity which paints the collectivity of females. In all of this we must delude ourselves that a Wall is the monopoly of the female. There can be a male **Bum-Bum Wall** which can be supremely vulgar. But this I have not yet seen.

Our declaration is that nakedness is immanently a cultural construct and has not a religious or spiritual consequence per se. In some societies eating with your hands is the norm and going to the toilet with your bottle of water is right and proper. Walking into your cubicle with your roll of toilet paper is anathema. Is the Bum- bum Wall an aberration or is it cultural or in the process of being cultural?

Our society at this time defines nakedness in terms of various parts or portion of the human anatomy; and in the female in particular, the pelvic area comes to the fore. In Carnival 2023, we saw displayed and exposed in most females the pelvic area; and that area was being gyrated with phenomenal sinuosity that intimated a degree of vulgarity. And that is where the problem lies. The infringement of taboos and laws were being flaunted in an environment of joyous lasciviousness; and that defined our Carnival for the greater part. Henceforth the **Bum-Bum Wall** will become a permanent feature of the Lucian Carnival and populist acceptance will become the norm.

In this year's Carnival, there were ten heterogenous musical bands, and the one that stood out in competitive array was The **Tribe of Twel**. Its conspicuousness propelled it into a category that in a way was not really modern Lucian Carnival. It was like comparing oranges and grapefruits: significantly close in phylum but qualitatively different in rectitude, respectability and acceptability.

Paradoxically, the two types helped to create a joyous occasion without complementing each other. The **"nine"** made their libation to **Bacchus**. The **Tribe of Twel**, their libation was to **Bacchus** and to **Sophia**. There lies the fundamental difference.

As I see it, **Tribe of Twel** is indeed deserving of my applause and that of all men and women of balanced judgement.

As I take my leave I would like to pose this question. It is simple but not simplistic, intriguing and thought provoking. It is this:

What do you think of a nudist camp/colony? Or in the alternative, have you visited, or will you visit a nudist colony/ camp?

CRIME AND THE FAMILY

At this time, Saint Lucia is virtually inundated with criminal activity of a felonious and heinous type. The incidence of homicide is alarming and on the increase, and unlawful personal injury seems to be a banal past-time in the resolution of contentious issues, particularly among the youth.

Solutions are being sought on official, informal and institutional levels, but yet the carnage continues unabated. The question is Why? We seek the rehabilitation of inmates, writ large, but to no avail. The fifteen year old commits murder as well as the thirty-five year old. And juxtaposed to the gruesome statistic is the venal, criminal commission by those who were never arraigned or incarcerated. Why this grotesque failure on this level? Is it because the society needs to be rehabilitated?

WE seem to need more and more police in whatever the mode and wherever situate. But isn't that indicative of a very glaring and alarming fact that the society itself is on a wrong path? We do have a certain confidence in our police force; but then it is not a blind and blinding confidence. For the resolution of our current problems it must never be.

As we have just indicated the society needs to be rehabilitated, and that implies that its constitutive elements, in isolation and plurality, need to be addressed. And one of the major and indispensable elements of this society is the **family unit**. That term in its essence implies cohesiveness and therefore is diametrically opposed to **crime** which on whatever the level, whatever its mode, whatever its manifestation and whatever its time, is **divisive**.

Family and **Crime** cannot co-exist; and the ascendancy of one is consequentially and aetiologically to the descendency of the other. Hence, it is imperative that attention at this time, and for the longevity and survival of the society, that attention be focused on the five-year old sitting on the school benches of this nation. Before he sits, he must be prepared to sit and it is this sitting process that engages in ascending order, **mother, father, school and church**. And it is on this level that the seeds of cohesiveness are sown. And it is **time** that determines whether the society reaps what it has sown or suffer the whirlwind in its disintegration.

It is the **family** that justifies our existence; it is the family that provides the *raison d'etre* for our being. Without the **family**, chaos and anarchy would prevail and our humanity recede into the abyss of crime and violence. And so, the structures and sub-structures that directly and indirectly impact on the **family** in its singularity and plurality must, at this time, urgently orient their formal and informal exertions toward the elevation and sublimation of the **family unit** in its diversity.

The immediacy of our rather morbid, nefarious situation seems to be the formal and official preoccupation in dealing with this scourge of crime. That is a mistake. The **church**, writ large, is there: somewhat somnolent with a pathetic, ineffective and occasional gasp of energy and intent. It has failed us. It too is inexorably linked with the **family** and has a dynamic role to play in the formation and transformation of the **family**. To the mundane it adds a vital spiritual element in the creation of a society that gives salubrious expression to this communion of the spiritual and the secular. And by so being nullifies the propensity towards the commission of the sins of avarice and hubris. These two and for the greater part are the constitutive elements of criminal behaviour.

It is to be noted that the family of today is characteristically different to the family of yesteryear; and it is this difference that validates the position that our present society needs to be rehabilitated. The perception of that need emanates from a bygone era and casts doubt on the instrumentality of what is needed. For the paradox that confronts us is simply this: how can we rehabilitate that which has not been habilitated? And that is the crux of the problem as far as our criminogenic youth is concerned. They emanate from the family of today where the youth have a cognitive discernment of what is wrong and what is right, what is good and what is evil, and what is vicious and what is benign.

But they do not have a **moral sensitivity** to that which is criminal and that which is not. There is a certain characterological dissonance between their moral sensibilities and their knowledge of good and evil. And so, the alarming thing is that they have the intelligence but not the morality. And as it has been said in times past, intelligence and morals are ethical, and an ethical being can make choices but among the choices are the things, the deeds that he or she will not do.

And so when a youth of nineteen years shoots another in the balcony of his home, or a sixteen year old girl fatally stabs her friend on the school grounds, that is not **immorality**; and when a youth shoots his drug partner, that is not a matter of **immorality**; and when a youth (12 years – 35 years) shoots someone through the window of his passing car at a crowded rum-shop and in consequence thereof a patron is coerced into surrendering, rather untimely, his mortality, that is not **immorality**; and when a girl at a secondary school sits at the front of her class with her thighs apart, and smilingly gives her male teacher an unobstructed view of her titillating and fascinating possibilities, that is not a matter of **immorality**.

At this time, this age, this era, these are not incidents of immorality. These are incidents emanating from within the bosom our present day family structure: **The Family**.

It is to be noted that **immorality** implies a certain grounding in moral values, moral dogmas, moral teachings that have become warped or tainted because of the negative vicissitudes of life; because of the struggles and conflicts between good and evil in a domestic, personal and thespian environment: the stage of life. **Immorality** is the breakdown of one's moral edifice, one's super-ego as they combat with the values-in-action of the society. It connotes the struggle passive or otherwise, with a residual consciousness of that which is good, positive wholesome, normative and sublime in one's social environment.

But then what we are faced with at this time, in this age, this era and in this place, and since the "shift systems", is not immorality but **AMORALITY. Amorality** among the youth (12 to 35) years to now. And so, a patent lack of conscience, be it social, spiritual or otherwise now defines the shift and quasi shift cohorts and the ensuing generation. **THE FAMILY**.

The management of the Past, Present and Future needs to be predicated on one sociological phenomenon that has been and is generating the whirlwind of Crime. This phenomenon is **AMORALITY.**

At this juncture, it is to be noted that besides the family there are other elements to be harnessed in the resolution of this crisis of **Crime.** Some of these are the **Church, the Police, the Unions, the Schools and all other community collectives.**

The Collective Dynamic is the solution. "For no Man is an island entire of itself. Every man's death diminishes me, because I am involved in mankind. And therefore never send to know for whom the bell tolls: it tolls for thee."

EGREGIOUS IRRESPONSIBILITY
(As I See It)

The United States of America at this time is the epicentre of the Covid-19 scourge. It has approximately 3.5 million of confirmed cases and, in conjunction therewith and as a consequence thereof, has regressed into a death ascending spiral of 136,000 persons.

The U.S. is perhaps the wealthiest country in the world; it is perhaps the most developed and technologically advanced country in the world. But is it the most advanced civilisation on this planet? It is being whispered that China is the force to be reckoned with and on a multiplicity of levels.

In spite of its laudable achievements in the area of health, in particular, this country is now the epicentre of the Covid-19 pandemic. Globally, it is now number one. A dubious distinction and achievement that indicate to me that there is an alarming flaw in the national psyche and characterological composition of the "American". And that composition embraces the elements of racism, hedonism, materialism and individualism that manifest themselves, and grotesquely so, in the personal conduct and policy postures of that persona. In its singularity the collectivity is reflected, and there one discerns flaws and cracks that betray the salubrious aspirations of an emerging and struggling morality. And it is that qualified morality and *modus vivendi* that have made that country so vulnerable in the face of Covid-19.

Why has the mighty USA been unable to deal with the Covid onslaught? Lesser endowed countries have attained varying measures of success in relation to the containment of this pandemic. Why is the mighty US failing? A country that is looked up to by many countries and peoples? It is an admired global power, but for what? The national image projected is that of a philanthropic, democratic society. It purports to define itself as the saviour of itself and of the world. But where is that saving grace in relation to Covid-19? What is it that the pandemic has revealed about the heart and soul of the "American"? Where are the values that are being espoused and extolled? A country reeling from the pandemic: a country virtually on its knees. What is the reality and why? Paradoxically, its existential posture is in some measure predicated on Love. But then Love is personal, individual and particular; and societally does it suffice? A corollary of Love is Charity and the two purports to be the *raison d'être* and *elan vitae* of this society's existence. Does that suffice? It does not and that is where the fundamental crack and flaws lie. And how many have fallen into that crack of self deception: an existential void. Therein lies the vulnerability of the "American".

Where is the Love, where is the Charity? They are both present. The "American" is revelling in a cauldron of Love and Charity but to the exclusion of that which is indispensable for human civilisation. And that is Justice. The "American is confusing and equating Love and Charity with Justice. And that is a fundamental error that inimically and deleteriously strike at the heart and soul of the "American". And so, in its putrid nudity, Covid-19 is exposing the absence of Justice: that core value that does not define the psyche of the "American".

On a very human level and in its plurality the greatest of all values is Justice in its teleological universality; and that is why the notion of Heaven and Hell is inextricably and eschatologically linked with it. Love on the other hand and in its genesis is celestial/spiritual and hence the reason why this enigma, how can a finite being in a finite situation, commit a finite act, with finite deliberateness and deserve infinite punishment "in the realm of human affairs loses its logical perplexity. Love in its inherent and numinous manifestation permeates the behavioural incidents that constitute the living processes and actions of homo sapiens. As has been said, we are both sinners and saints and that is the central ambiguity of the human condition. And so instead of accepting the two, the "American" is endeavouring to resolve the two as opposites and which is indeed a conceptual error.

At this juncture you my dear reader may now posit the question that lies in abeyance in the recesses of your inquiring mind. What is the nexus between the catastrophe of Covid-19 and **"Egregious Irresponsibility"**? One must then allude to the hereinbefore conditions of racism, hedonism, materialism and individualism and juxtaposing these to the value of Justice which is qualified and varied in its limited absence in the "American". And so whatever the exalted pronouncement and declarations that he makes in his historical march through time there is a behavioural disjunction and attitudinal dissonance that make him a threat to the generalised societal other. And we here in Saint Lucia are part of that other.

That is the **threat** that brings into disturbing and disconcerting focus the **opening up of our borders** to the "American" at this time of Covid-19. One hundred and fifty thousand of the "American" have effected their terrestrial demise. Their death for the greater part could have been avoided or prevented. Money, other resources, and intellect, did not prevent that calamity, that tragedy and why? Deaths that occurred within their borders, their homes their castles and hospitals, their cities, their towns and villages. So many fell into their own characterological crack, abyss, lacunae by their own doings and undoings. A crack with its own unappreciated suicidal propensity has been devastating.

WE on this paradise of an island do not seem to be alarmed when we should be. We have become blinded by our secular, mundane concerns and desires and have lost sight of that which should be of intrinsic value to us as Lucians. The fatal failings of the "American" should have alerted us or put us on the alert. That does not seem to be the case. And so a decision was made on our behalf and with our connivance and complicity to open our borders to the "American". We did not object nor did we demonstrate.

Will we with the effluxion of time be reaping the whirlwind ???

In all of this I see Egregious Irresponsibility.

HAIR, HERE AND THERE

A school is an institution and for its existence, purpose, longevity and goals it must have rules and regulations that constitute its Code of Conduct.

In short, it must have Discipline; and discipline cannot be singular: it must be catholic or universal in its applicability and enforcement.

In any institution, there must be a hierarchy of rules and regulations, which in their enforcement, imports varying degrees of "punishment" writ large. For example, verbal warning, written warning, caning, suspension (with or without remuneration) and ultimately expulsion or dismissal.

To invoke any of these, the infringement must be contextualised in relation to the fundamental goal and raison d'être of the institution.

In relation to St. Mary's College and other schools, the issue at this time and in this instance, the issue is tonsorial. Hair is Here and There. And so the question that needs to be asked is, what is the function and purposeful nexus between "scalpel: hair wherever and however situate and any of the hierarchical goals of the institution? For example, grooming, hygiene etc.

If these two are juxtaposed to the fundamental goal or goals of the institution, and which is producing educated and law abiding citizens, one can discern a certain qualitative disparity that imports degrees of punitive responses that are commensurate.

With this tonsorial issue/problem, universality of prohibition or prescription must come to the fore. Whatever the rule or regulation, it must be promulgated in its specificity or varied modality.

Contextually speaking, the promulgation of regulations (writ large) should be in written form and transmitted to each student and his or her household. This would obviate the possibility of ignorance being in the service of knowledgeability and enlightenment. And by a parent being surprised by the disciplinary action taken by the institution in relation to a student.

As already indicated, "punishment" meted out must be in conformity the body of rules and regulations of the institution and must be anything but draconian in its elasticity.

Rules and Regulations, Codes of Conduct must be FAIR. And Fairness can only be ascertained in terms of the fundamental goal and mission of the institution in its specificity, universality and enlightened applicability.

And so the relevant and germane question is, what kind of response?

It must be a response that is in conformity and commensurate with one or more of the hierarchy of Rules and Regulations of the College and ultimately aligned with the fundamental goal and mission of the school.

Generically speaking, the ultimate Goal and Mission of a School/ College is to produce educated and law-abiding citizens.

LUCIAN POLITICS AMONG THE DOCTORS

Philosophy has been dethroned, and Enlightenment and Naivety embraced in a grotesque dance for survival in the politics of the absurd. That is Lucian politics.

While lying on my bed of sleep this past Thursday evening (11th March 2021) my mind was assailed by a multiplicity of questions that shot out of the Richard/St.Rose TV exchange. It was interesting, revealing and somewhat perplexing. It screamed for questions to be answered by the conspicuously absent Choiseul "constituents".

What was the mechanism used to facilitate the emergence of the hitherto unknown Dr. Pro? Was there a run-off? Was there a poll? In what way did "700" became the magic number and representative of the SLP voting electorate? Whatever the mechanism, was it predicated on the principles of democracy and transparency?

I do not have the answers which at this time and stage would have enabled me to accept or reject the conflicting positions of the good and aspiring doctors. With that level of ignorance staring me in the face I must necessarily address my mind to the seemingly principled posture assumed by the good male doctor. Is he right to stand on principle whatever that principle is? The answer of course is Yes.

One must always hold on to principle particularly in the resolution of conflicting issues. For as has been said, principle is either wholly kept or wholly sacrificed and that the slightest concession on matters of principle implies the abandonment of principle. And the doctor is a principled man. Principle indeed makes the man or woman and its derogation facilitates the slippage into venality and opportunism.

And so these questions arise. Contextually speaking, is it pragmatic for the good doctor to stand on principle? Can principle and pragmatism co-exist? Where do ethics and integrity come in? Is situational ethics the cop-out in this contrived drama? Is it the solution to this existential conflict? And can the good doctor's honour survive? There is so much that is unknown.

Is the good lady also standing on principle? If that is indeed the case then the truth in this drama of ambition is being sacrificed or compromised. Who is being economical with the truth and therefore is motivated by greed in the commission of the sin of hubris? Assuming that what the good doctor is asserting is indeed the truth then the process of choice was flawed. And if that is indeed so then the Party including its Leader were complicit in the selection process. Then that puts to question the individual and collective of so many. A very frightening situation.

I do not know the good doctor: but I think I know Philip J Pierre. I am prepared to accept that which he supported and gave his blessing. And in fairness to the good doctor I am prepared to accept the very real probability that he was mistaken or misled.

As has been said, politics is the art of the possible and the core mission in this enterprise is to assume the governance of a country. To win a general election is the primary *raison d'être* of a political party and the second isto effectuate plans, programs and policies to the satisfaction of the electorate. It is a collective endeavour that embraces the collectivity. No one person can achieve that goal whether in terms of his own constituency or the country as a whole. And the passion that drives a man or a woman to enter the realm of politics is not self interest, enlightened or otherwise, but patriotism.

"Ask Not what your country can do for you but what you can do for your country."

In this erudite, talented and empathetic doctor I see (and others do) an excellent Minister of Health. Apart from Finance, the most important portfolio in government. From my vantage point I see a certain probability: almost certainty that should be considered by him not in terms of his own personal elevation or aggrandisement but in terms of the noble impulse (patriotism) that has propelled him into the arena of politics.

Again, as I see it, the good doctor has an important contribution to make in the development of this country and its people. His present course would be tantamount to a betrayal of all of us and a condemnation of all of us; for we would be condemned to languish in a society ,on an island, where criminal political mismanagement would be the order of the day, the month, the years, the decades. A frightening and alarming situation for my grand children and theirs.

Good Doctor!!! The best amongst us have concluded that for you a three cornered fight would be suicidal in terms of who and what you are, in terms of your potential and also in terms of what would constitute the justification of your existence. You would have two opponents to defeat: **two institutions**. The winner in this three cornered fight is he or the entity that controls the policy making mechanism in this insular political sphere. You do not feature... regardless.

Indeed you are an honourable man and so it behoves you to do the honourable thing that takes into consideration your very human fallibility.

Seven hundred (700) Frenchmen could be wrong.

What pellucidly must be understood is that life in its unfolding mode and evolution is not linear. It is at times convoluted with its highs and lows evidencing situations of righteous and valid conflicts that give rise to what may be termed as the hierarchy of values that constitutes and defines the principles that guide and guard the incidents of living as we as human beings explore our varied action space. In terms of the hierarchy of values, what the good doctor needs to address himself to is that which can be perceived as the greater good. That which is in the best interest of the totality, the whole.

A certain validity and justification may be perceived sectorally but then what does the **big picture** indicate? And is the part greater than the whole? The optimal manifestation or expression of principle can only be in terms of its holistic consequence and not in relation to a constituent part of the whole. What the good doctor must do, and as he has intimated, must be consonant with principle and in the circumstance of humanity, since we all expect him to do the honourable thing for the **greater good**.

In closing, I reiterate the admission that in relation to this matter I know essentially nothing except the fact of my ignorance which highlights in my litigious and disputatious mind the obvious requirement of **evidence**.

This is not a matter of contradictions and conflicts that assail us; that punctuate our daily lives. It is a matter of principle and morality. A defining but simple choice between that which is right and that which is wrong.

PAROLE

This "piece" was written or perhaps re-written more than a year ago but was never published; but since I perceive a certain relevance in terms of what presently obtains I have decided to promulgate my thinking on this matter of parole as conceptualised a long time ago.

On the **28th November 1997**, THE PAROLE ACT (No.12/1997) became the law of the land. Its birth and seeming demise coincided with that date, for up to the time of penning these words, this piece of legislation has never been operationalised. As a Bill, it had been debated in the House and was therefore scrutinised and analysed in the Senate. And so, the question that comes to the fore is, why having been enshrined in our jurisprudence, this Act was allowed to languish in a comatose state?

Considering the temper of the times and the exigencies of our criminal justice situation and the burgeoning population at Bordelais, why hasn't the Parole Act been considered at this time? In very recent times five inmates of that institution have had their period of incarceration terminated before the normal expiration of their judicially temporal constraint. They had not fully served their years of incarceration but they were released through the instrumentality of the Committee on the Prerogative of Mercy.

That Committee falls under Section 74 of our Constitution and it reads in part:

"The Governor General may:

(a) *Grant a pardon, either free or subject to lawful conditions, to any person convicted of any offence...*

Remit the whole or any part of any punishment

Imposed on any person for any offence or of any penalty or forfeiture otherwise due to the Crown on account of any offence."

The power and authority that devolve upon the Governor General are informed by the Committee on the Prerogative of Mercy, which is composed of, and at most, six persons. These are in part, a Minister of Government, the Attorney General and the Chief Medical Officer. And so, as regards the five inmates that were released from prison Section 74 (d) was actuated. Regrettably, the terms of imprisonment and the nature of the offences were not disclosed. That information, in my opinion, should have been promulgated so that we the public would have been better positioned to assess the process and rectitude of the decision. As I see it, transparency in the exercise of governmental power, on whatever the level, is a *sine qua non* for effective, salubrious democratic governance.

From the paucity of information received, what I have gleaned is that the five inmates were released because:

1. they were considered to have been rehabilitated,
2. they no longer posed a threat to the society; and
3. their length of incarcerated time was deemed sufficient considering their individual circumstance.

At this time, Bordelais, with over 500 inmates is alarmingly overcrowded. And five hundred inmates minus five do not in any way resolve that sardine-can problem. But then, the resolution of that problem has never been the focus and raison d'être of the Committee. As of 2019, ten inmates, contextually speaking, were released; in 2003, one, and in 2005, three. In 2006, one, in 2015, one and in 2016, five. The overcrowding problem had not been addressed but the Committee had served its purpose.

Overcrowding militates against the aims and objectives of the Bordelais institution in many ways. It creates a security problem; it subverts the various modalities of rehabilitation and prostitutes the Human Rights of the imprisoned population not only in terms of their sequestered environment but also in terms of their anticipated and successful reintegration into the society.

What then is needed is a *modus operandi* and *modus vivendi* that are predicated upon the enlightened constraints of legislative fiat. And in this regard the Parole Act comes to the fore. At this time, our Parole Act is either dead, dying or comatose.

At this time it is quite germane to pose the question: what is Parole? Section 2 of the said Act provides the answer. It states:

"Parole means the authority granted to release a prisoner under the Act from prison in which he is serving a sentence and under supervision of a Parole Officer be permitted to spend the remainder of that sentence out of prison."

Falling under the rubric of this Act are two Administrative structures: the Parole Board and the Parole Committee. The primary function of the Board is to receive and consider applicants for parole and to grant or reject such applications. The function of the Committee is to make recommendations to the Board for consideration as a result of any investigation carried out by it.

As regards the issue of eligibility, every prisoner serving a sentence of more than twelve months shall be eligible for parole after having served a period of one third of such a sentence of twelve months, which ever is the greater. However, it is to be noted in Section 6 that a prisoner who has been sentenced for life or in respect of whom a sentence of death has been commuted for life shall be eligible for parole after having served a period of not less than fifteen years.

Parole does not stop at the exit portal of the prison. It continues into the community and engages various ministries of government, civil society and society generally. Certain structures need to be put into place to effectuate the salubrious objective of parole; and linkages must be established to facilitate the life and living of the parolee in his community, adopted or otherwise. First, there must be a cadre of Parole Officers to supervise the parolee while on parole. One or two half-way houses must be established to provide temporary housing and shelter for the parolee, who on being paroled most likely has no available place of abode. Further, the half-way house facilitates a gentle and gradual entry or re-entry into his new environment.

From the Parole Office, linkages must be established with commercial houses so that job opportunities can be made available or capitalised upon. Generally, the society needs to be educated as to the *raison d'être* and rationale of a parole program. Each sector of the society has its role to play in preventing the parolee from becoming a recidivistic static.

As I see it, the overcrowding at Bordelais needs to be urgently addressed. One third of five hundred is about one hundred and sixty-six, and that is a significant number. Therein lies the solution for this institutional overcrowding. And it is a solution that embraces the rehabilitative thrust of this institution. Without a functioning PAROLE ACT in an environment peculiar to its societal exigencies, the incidence of crime will never meaningfully be reduced. Its omission and disregard in our day to day rehabilitation exertions since 1977 has been egregious and deserving of the obloquy of our time.

In the final analysis it must be noted that without a formal institution for rehabilitation our Criminal Justice System would grind to a halt. For antecedent to the process of rehabilitation is the process of Sentencing. And the Courts in Criminal matters must upon conviction, sentence. That virtually is the fundamental reason for the existence of the Criminal Court since the fundamental principle of sentencing is the protection of the Society; and the Society includes the offender.

And so ,as I conclude my criminological ruminations it must pellucidly be postulated that the triad of our National Security consists of the Police, the Prison and the Society, civilly. There will always be criminal activity; and though the primary way to reduce crime is to focus on the Police, a fully operational PAROLE SYSTEM will go a long way in making Bordelais a more viable, functional and effective institution for national security and social rehabilitation.

I have written a few more "pieces" including Crime and the Police. These I will publish, perhaps, in the fullness of time; my time.

Parting words of enlightenment: Laws do not stop or prevent crime and so the journey has only just begun.

THE PIAYE SAGA

Was it **Sand Mining** or **Desilting**? That is disjunctive. Was it sand mining and not desilting? Was it desilting and not sand mining? Seeming confusion. So what really happened at the Piaye Beach? In their initial statement at whatever the time and place, Minister Bradley used the term **Desilting** in relation to whatever was going on at Piaye. He even informed us as to what this activity entailed and its purpose. At no time did he use the word **sand mining**.

"Champagne," a party hack (and my definition of a party hack is someone, contextually speaking, who supports a political party and in the process of so doing suspends his intellectual processes – I am cognisant of the implied presumption), in his initial statement or comment, used the term **Desilting**. Thirdly, the "Bowtie Man" in the same context used the term **Desilting**. Among the three and initially the term **Sand mining** was conspicuous by its. absence. In relation to the three musketeers, the terms conspirators, aiders and abettors, accomplices and collaborators come to mind. At least one description is. applicable.

As this saga unfolded, the Chief Engineer attached to the Ministry of Infrastructure naively, inadvertently or honestly made this revelation, declaration or disclosure that Minister Bradley had at some relevant time requested a permit or licence on behalf of himself or others for **Sand mining** at the Piaye Beach and not at the confluence of the Piaye river and the ocean.

What was observed on site was huge, monstrous heavy equipment perched on top of tons and tons of excavated sand. The mouth of the Piaye River could not produce that amount of sand. A further observation were piles and piles of tons and tons of sand not too far away. And so the question that needs to be asked, was this **Sand mining** or **Desilting?** It may be true that common sense may not be as common as we expect it to be; But the common wisdom of the plebeian herd would of necessity and logically draw it to the ineluctable conclusion that that activity at the Piaye Beach was indeed Sand mining.

At a later date and in a futile endeavour to explain away his predicament, Minister Bradley stated that the terms **Sand mining** and **Desilting** in common usage were interchangeable: they were one and the same. And when initially he used the term **Desilting** he also could have meant **Sand mining**.

Just ponder this scenario. If I stood on the beach, Vigie that is, before the Terminal with 20 drums and began filing them up, would I be engaged in **Desilting** or **Sand mining?** Or would I be doing both according to Minister Bradley? If I went to the Roseau Dam with a *bako*[5] and began moving the sand on the river bed that feeds water into the dam would I be Sand mining or **Desilting**? What must be noted is that there is a situational and geographic distinction between the two activities. The distinction or substantive and beyond the qualitative. A lemon and a lime are they one and the same?

At this junction the question that comes to mind is why Minister Bradley "initially" used the term **Desilting**? What was the **motivation**? The Minister, like myself, is a very educated man, so why this seeming confusion? Was he really confused or mistaken when he initially used the term **Desilting**? I do not think that the Minister was confused or mistaken. This may be a strange juxtaposition, but I see a probable nexus between that motivation and another instance where his **motivation** gives me cause for pause. The initial use of **Desilting was deliberate**. That is my conclusion/opinion.

This **instance** brings to mind the **DSH**[6] debacle. This Agreement was executed in part by Minister Bradley and the Prime Minister in their official capacity. Subsequent thereto, Minister Bradley made

---

5 Saint Lucian parlance for, "backhoe".

6 DSH Caribbean Star Limited - Framework Agreement)

the admission that he signed the document before reading it – in part or in whole – and was not aware of certain disturbing, disconcerting and prejudicial provisions in that document when that document found itself in the public domain.

This Agreement, on paper at least, would revolutionise positively and negatively the quality of life of the people of the South. As I stated earlier Minister Bradley is a very educated man particularly in the area of Finance and Banking. And so, why would he sign that Agreement, and according to his own admission, without reading it in its totality? A document that virtually would disenfranchise the people of the South. An Agreement that in its operationalisation would be tantamount to the rape of Saint Lucia (Helen of Troy, the face that launched a thousand ships. Helen, the wife of Menaulus, not being raped by Paris of Helenistic Greece but our Helen of the West being gang raped by "our people" and a scoundrel from the East.)

Did that educated man sign that Agreement without reading it? As an educated man, my position is simply this: this educated Minister did read the Framework Agreement before he signed it. And this brings me to the issue of **motivation**. Why did he sign the **DSH Framework Agreement?**

Minister Bradley has many attributes. He is gregarious, pleasant, affable perspicacious and of course educated. But is he cunning? **I am not, and also not a Jack-ass**

THE HUG THAT ROCKED THE WORLD

With a spiritual act of courage and in his magnificent humility, Brandt Jean conferred upon himself and his deceased brother, Botham Jean, immortality in the circumstance of humanity. All of this is circumscribed by these words:

"If you truly are sorry, I know I can speak for myself, I forgive you. I love you as a person...I know that if you go to God and ask Him, he will forgive you...I don't know if this is possible, but can I give her a HUG please? Please?"

The question was posed to the Judge and she responded in the affirmative. And from his seat in the witness box Brandt Jean walked towards the killer/murderer of his twenty six (26) year old brother, Botham Jean. It was a short walk and she stumblingly met him half way.

It must have been the hardest walk in his life and at the same time, because of who and what he was, it was the easiest. It reminded me of this young man who walked two hundred (200) yards to his cross of death two thousand plus years ago; and for Him it was the easiest and most joyful experience in his rather short life. He was thirty three (33) years old. The two events that traversed the silent legions of miles and years shared a numinous commonality in that Love and Forgiveness were the sublime and celestial provenance of it all.

He, the Black man, in his humble magnificence walked towards the White woman, the killer of his brother. She who wantonly destroyed the dreams, the aspirations, the hopes and the domestic life of this Lucian family, was embraced. He hugged her and she sobbingly hugged him.

It is an event the world will never forget. And from this day forward, in churches, synagogues, mosques and temples where the virtues of Love and Forgiveness are being taught, discussed and pontificated upon, Brandt Jean shall be the reference point to the faithful and even the heathen.

And to those who want to disparage the words and actions of this young man, it is their conscious and unconscious hypocrisy that is being given utterance on whatever the level. And further, their perverse expression is a grotesque manifestation of their dubious concern for the Jean family.

As regards Amber Guyger, I am of the opinion that she was racist like so many of her associates. But Guyger did not leave her place of work to head to her home and to kill a Black man. But a Black man died; he died, was shot, was murdered because of a concatenation of negative attitudinal events and bad luck that can only be surmised. If Botham was white, very likely he would not have been shot; but Guyger's mindset of a traditional and historical cast predisposed her to pull the trigger of her gun. And which she did.

The woman who was convicted for the murder of Botham Jean was indeed guilty of murder. And her punishment as I see it should have been thirty years of incarceration. But that was not to be. Interestingly, if she had gotten thirty years, Brandt's Hug and his declaration of Love would have lost some of its import, its significance. Ten (10) years enhanced augmented and sublimated to the spiritual this disposition of Love and Forgiveness.

From my study of human nature on certain levels I have come to the conclusion that Amber Guyger, up to the time she made that walk to Brandt Jean, was an Amber Guyger her family and friends knew. But the Amber Guyger who walked the forty-eight (48) feet towards Brandt Jean, that held him, that embraced him, that HUGGED him, was a different Amber Guyger. Along that stretch of floor something happened. She went through a catharsis that occasioned a characterological metamorphosis on a very profound level. She was reborn. And many who witnessed this phenomenon were themselves changed in varying degrees.

Forgiveness changes both the forgiver and the forgiven.

Love changes both the lover and the loved.

Love and Forgiveness, they are both one and the same though paradoxically the former is the genesis of the latter.

The Brothers: In death and in Life they have both justified each other's existence and the world is a better place because of them.

As I end this piece, I leave with you this thought with its aetiological implications and which of course is a product of my philosophical ruminations:

The Absolute and Quintessential manifestation of Love is to Forgive the Unrepentant.

THE METAPHYSICS OF CORRUPTION

Corruption is a perverse, universal and debilitating phenomenon that reflects, in some measure, the essential finitude of homo sapiens. It is an aberration that is in contradiction to the construct of perfection, and as such, is a necessity in the very process of creation. Its aetiology reposes in the human condition that in itself is consequent and immanent to the process of "becoming" as opposed to "being".

"Being" is and therefore is sempiternal. Perfection is not the quintessence of "becoming". Perfection is and therefore is eternal. "Being" and Perfection constitute an eternal reality that embraces all that which has not been created. And so all that which is "being" is perfect and that which is perfect is "being". Homo sapiens is anything but; and so his or her condition of existence reflects propensities that are either sublimating or demeaning. And that brings to the fore the notion, the issue of Choice.

Choice is not human in its provenance: it transcends that, as it ensures our humanity. Without this faculty of choice Homo Sapiens would not exist. He could not decide since his or her decision making process is predicated upon the faculty of choice. And so with choice the genesis of alternatives becomes manifest with its immanent inequalities that are discerned by his evolving rationality.

Corruption is the epiphenomenon of this inequality and therefore is a perennial facet of human existence. It is a condition of living but not an existential imperative. Man is not born to be evil. He or she is not born to be corrupt. Within the core of his or her being corruption lies in potency, to be activated by the exercise of the power of choice.

Man, Woman choose to be corrupt and it is his or her existential circumstance that provides the template for the emergence or reification of his or her acts of corruption. And for these acts he or she as a rational entity, is responsible. Only that which is rational can be endowed with the faculty of choice and thus rationality can be a double edged instrument of benevolence or venality.

Homo sapiens is not corrupt, but he has the capacity to be corrupt. He or she can live a life of immaculate rectitude, be a paragon of virtue but on the other hand the incidents that constitute the totality of his living impulses can be a checkered fabric with slots of rectitude and corruption, in varying degrees of prominence. If he or she is corrupt it is because he or she chooses to be so and thus making himself or herself accountable for the consequences of his or her acts of corruption. And accountability is not a mere abstraction but an essential reality upon which Justice in its various forms and modes, is predicated. Hence corruption does not exist in a moral vacuum but is inextricably and consequentially aligned with the notion of punishment.

Corruption exists in behavioural space peculiar to homo sapiens. For example, it exists in political space and for the greater part it defines that space. Hence the ubiquitous observation and experience that most politicians are corrupt. They are not corrupt metaphysically but are corrupt on a banal, mundane and deprecating level of human existence.

Rene Descartes' Cartesian Doubt comes to mind: "Cogito Ergo sum"[7]. Or should the correct postulation be, "I am therefore I think"?. However, philosophically couched the principles emanating there from can, in my opinion, be extrapolated to the phenomenon of corruption particularly when juxtaposed to the politics of our time.

I am anything but a mathematician, but another latin phrase comes to mind. It is this: *"Quod erat demonstratum"*. Do you see the connection?

Incidentally, Descartes was both a philosopher and mathematician. From the grains of my thoughts you may discern a pearl of wisdom and of truth.

---

[7] "I think therefore I am"

THE HOLE

For the past weeks and months the public on a multiplicity of levels of ignorance had to deal with what I choose to term as **"the Letter of Guarantee"**. It involves the company known as PAJOAH LIMITED and our Minister of Economic Development etc. I have not heard the Minister state, and categorically so, that he is not the author of that letter, which at this time is in the public domain. His statements of obfuscation and irrelevance have only led me to come and reasonably so, to the ineluctable conclusion that he, the Minister, authored that letter. That letter was written/typed on the Minister's official letter-head and had affixed to it what purports to be the Minister's signature. In the parlance of the pavement, if it waddles like a duck, quacks like a duck and excretes like a duck, then it should be a duck. But then, we live in a strange world where fake news is the new reality and truth is what one believes the truth to be. Relativity ethics exalted and assuming a rather grotesque posture.

As I see it in this miasma of "truth" and "fake news" there is one question in its quintessential simplicity that needs to be asked. And it is this: **was or is the Minister the author of that letter?** Regardless of the paucity of one's erudition, the question would not be cerebrally difficult to formulate. And its monosyllabic response would be even less tasking: **YES / NO**. If the Minister's response is in the negative, that is he was not or is not the author of that letter then a further question comes to the fore, and it is this: **Who forged the Minister's signature?**

It is to be noted that Forgery is a very serious offence (see Sections 235 et al) that on a defendant's conviction a term of imprisonment of two years is the minimum sentence. If that letter was forged, it would be incumbent on the Prime Minister to effectuate a police investigation immediately that would have punitive judicial consequences. **Somebody would have to go to jail.** And in this context where National Security would be compromised only incarceration would suffice as a deterrent. For no Minister and even the Prime Minister would feel safe knowing that there is someone out there who could and forge the signature of a Minister. The consequence of this would be that all government processes would have to be circumscribed by several layers and levels of protection and security. A very costly exercise.

But, if on the other hand, that " **Letter of Guarantee**" was authored by the Minister, and he has so admitted, then the Prime Minister and even we the people are faced with a situation trust. In his dubious comments in explicating the substance of that letter I heard the honourable gentleman alluding to the sins of commission and omission of the previous government going back almost to the Neanderthal past: Juffali, Grynberg, Rochamel, Linquist, to name a few. That, in my opinion constitutes an insult to my intelligence, for all of this is grossly irrelevant. There is one and only one issue: **WHO IS THE AUTHOR OF THAT LETTER?**

If that letter was indeed written by the Minister then it is incumbent on the Prime Minister to discipline the Minister for usurping his power and authority, creating a situation where the economy of the country could negatively be impacted upon, for bringing the government into disrepute since possible situations of money laundering on a governmental level could have been created, and for subverting the fiduciary relationship that should exist between a Minister and the people of the country that he serves. That authorship is indeed a criminal lapse on the part of the Minister or any Minister and the course of discipline that the Prime Minister should embark upon must be commensurate with the level of discipline imposed on the person who forges the signature of a Minister. With the former, a term of imprisonment, with the Minister, expulsion from Cabinet. If indeed the letter was authored by the Minister, then another interesting and disturbing question is this: **for what purpose?**

At this time and considering the effluxion of time and the gravity of the matter the impotence of the Prime Minister is indeed disconcerting and even alarming.

Has a police investigation begun, that is if it is a **NO** scenario? If it is a **YES** scenario, why hasn't the Minister been disciplined? Is it because there is a perverse but functional relationship between these two men?

In relation to the Minister as the seeming or possible author, there is a disturbing and disconcerting situation that needs to be addressed by the people and the government as soon as possible. It is the situation of **"THE HOLE"** which is circumscribed by the word **"malfeasance". And all governments have been complicit in the creation of that hole, that chasm, that lacuna, that abyss.** And it is a "hole" that facilitates the alleged conduct of the alleged Minister; a hole filled with skeletons of corruption from the present and the past. How can that type of conduct be prevented if it is not enshrined in our Criminal Code? That conduct as I have intimated is Malfeasance and it contextually can be defined as:

"A wrongful act which a public officer has no legal right to do, or the doing of an act which a public officer ought not to do at all".

At this time, I challenge the Prime Minister to enact criminal legislation that covers this **hole of malfeasance**. And I further challenge the Leader of the Opposition to give the people of this country the assurance that when he assumes the governance of this country, the conduct of **Malfeasance** will be included in our

Criminal Code, for by so doing he will establish the template upon which all the processes of government will be predicated upon, and at last, **honest government** will be the societal norm. The people deserve that.

As an instructive note my definition of a "party hack" is the supporter of a political party who in the exercise of his dubious freedom and independence abdicates his integrity, objectivity and morality.

I am not a party hack.

THE NEW PARADIGM

Indeed we are in the "silly season", and with it the prostitution of our democratic ethos: the template upon which our franchise, contextually speaking, is being given at this time a perverse expression in a dubious quest for responsible national governance. It is election time and partisan politics rears its ugly head.

And howling in a cage of platforms for a change that is stultifying in its macabre impotency. And the amazing thing is that there is change without change as the various actors in their thespian roles delude the bovine populace time and time again.

In this political quagmire governance is a promise of fools for fools; a mirage on the desert of the people's expectation and a figment of one's imagination. As I see it, governance is a sublime and functional reality. It is, since its absence is an adjectival negativity, and hence falls within the realm of a macabre nihilism that is perfidious and crassly disappointing.

It is indeed the "silly season" and yet so many are oblivious to its futility and its purposelessness. Its characteristic and mundane feature is "de party"; whether red, yellow, blue or white. Colours without colour for a purpose they do not serve. For the colours we paint our hearts with are without the input of the mind. A somewhat atavistic posture of convenience, the genesis of which lies in a primordial, familial and genealogical association devoid of reason and ideological trappings.

And so the elements of "de party" vote in a blind frenzy of dubious and opportunistic allegiance. For whom or for what? The process is both divisive in its current mode and expression, and is futile in its intended purpose. The process is demeaning and banality is exalted. What really is being sought is governance that resounds to the benefit of the people on a multiplicity of levels. But what presently obtains is anathema to the attainment of governance, since the people do not intellectually engage themselves in the process and mechanism of choice.

Caught up in the cacophony of sounds and the meretricious melody of the platform rhetoric, they like sheep in orgasmic, venereal ecstasy erect the cross for their own crucifixion.

And so, with the effluxion of time we hear the drums of their individual and collective frustration and disappointments. What is needed is a revolution in thought, a departure from what presently obtains: a new PARADIGM. For it need to be pellucidly understood that it is the Government that creates the heaven and the hell. It is the Government that imposes the taxes: it is the Government that is corrupt: it is the Government that is not transparent; it is the Government that is not accountable.

It is indeed the Government in its collectivity and not the individual Ministers. And so the focus must be on the Government. The Government despite its profound abstraction is the reality. The Opposition is merely a package of promises, possibilities, probabilities suggestion, platitudes and uncertainties wallowing in a morass of faith and hope: amorphous, tenuous and nebulous in its proclaimed intentions. At election time it is the Government that needs to be tested: that must be tested. How should that test be crafted?

As I see it, what should be brought into existence is what I choose to term as the TEN NATIONAL IMPERATIVES and to which is attached a mark of 10 individually. In their totality they would result in a percentage mark of one hundred (100). These National Imperatives are:

Honesty (10); Visionary (10); Transparency (10); Enlightenment (10); Fairness (10); Accountability (10); Pragmatic (10); Decisiveness (10); Boldness (10); Humility (10).

This is the yardstick with or by which the Government should be measured. It is never the District Representative that creates the conditions that impact on your lives negatively or positively. It is always the Government and that Government is accountable to you.

And so at the witching time of night and in the presence of your presence you place the Government against the yardstick of the Ten National Imperatives. Only then are you prepared to vote intelligently. The passing grade is 51, and the fifties is sheer mediocrity.

With such a system in place, and as your guide the "silly season" would no longer be silly. It would be replaced by a salubrious atmosphere of individual and collective responsibility. The divisiveness, the acrimony and the violence on whatever the level would be relegated to the trash heap of historical oddities. The change would be real and meaningful and Saint Lucia and you the people would be responsible for this sublimating metamorphosis.

The interesting and remarkable consequence of all of this in the election scenario is that if the Government attains a failing mark then you simply support the individuals who are presented to you as opposition. Individuals whose character, capacities, potential and achievements that you know. If ignorance prevails on those levels then you assume the posture of the Silent Spectator.

As I conclude this presentation the thought and question that has filtered through my mind is this: shouldn't the pass mark be a rigorous 60% since it is the lives, the dreams, aspirations, hopes and potential of the people that are involved. Perhaps it should.

Some food for thought.

THE QUINTESSENCE OF ASININITY

A few weeks ago, the University of the West Indies announced that it was Antigua & Barbuda and not Saint Lucia that would be the locus in quo for the establishment of the 4th UWI campus in CARICOM.

The two countries were named; and so the question that needs to be asked, is why? Obviously, the two countries were in contention for what, in my opinion, should be a coveted achievement. Why did Saint Lucia lose? Why did all of us lose? These questions must be asked because this generation and succeeding generations have lost and on a multiplicity of levels.

Listening to the Minister articulate her pathetic, insulting and asinine explanation left me flabbergasted, dumbfounded and profoundly disappointed. We the people were expected to accept this explanation delivered in a manner where her mien and carriage depicted an inspissated arrogance. This opportunity should have been given the highest priority since its realisation or reification would have functionally and salubriously impacted on this society in its diverse dimension and aspect.

With the establishment of this campus here in Saint Lucia, the following would be some of the spinoffs and benefits that would accrue:

(a) Over the years the cost of university schooling would be reduced.

(b) There would be an increase of the student population from abroad.

(c) An increase in the positive economic impact in terms of homes being rented and the associated domestic expenditure of students.

(d) The marketing of the island from a touristic point of view would be enhanced and augmented.

(e) There would be the enhancement of our intellectual environment by its linkage with the Nobel Laureate phenomenon.

(f) The national pride and prestige of the island would soar far beyond our pedestrian expectations.

Having listened to the Minister, one would have to conclude that the Government was not interested in having the 4th UWI campus established here in Saint Lucia. And so the question that comes to the fore is this: Did the government via its Minister of Education convey to the administration of the University of the West Indies that Saint Lucia was not an interested party and that its focus and priority were to provide a grounding for the Sir Arthur Lewis Community College. That in my opinion is lopsided thinking even when one takes into consideration our present "open campus" with its limited intellectual reach, scope and depth. "My empire for a donkey" but we still hold on to the donkey.

Obviously, this was a competition; so why would Saint Lucia deliberately create the situation whereby Antigua & Barbuda win by default and Saint Lucia loses by its patent lack of vision and perspicacity. Being the 4th campus would have complimented our laureate experience and achievement. And the new designation would have established the nexus between Sir Arthur and the Honourable Derek. Voila! Here stands in its salubrious magnificence, the LEWIS WALCOTT UWI CAMPUS in SAINT LUCIA.

Because of an inept and visionless government, Saint Lucia has lost an extraordinary opportunity. We, who at one time, was the gem of the OECS and the apotheosis of our intellectual development, have been mortified, and are now the nadir of the region's scholastic index. We did not deserve this. But what we now deserve is the obloquy of this and future generations. The Minister of Education at least should be asked to resign. This debacle happened on her watch; and though others prominently but grotesquely misplayed their part in this tragedy, she most unfortunately and disappointingly fumbled the ball.

IT IS TO BE NOTED THAT THE SILENCE CONCERNING THIS MATTER IS DEAFENING.

THE SACRIFICIAL LAMB

Within its constitutional parameters much has been said and written about the Position of Deputy Speaker and its particular relevance or obsolescence at this Juncture in our dubious political evolution.

Some of our pundits have pontificated that there is no need for a Deputy Speaker and that only a Speaker suffices. Others hold that there is a qualified need for a Deputy Speaker and whose appointment or election is a matter of circumstantial necessity.

From the onset, what needs to be pellucidly comprehended is that the CONSTITUTION is the Supreme Law of the State. Section 120 reads:

> **"This Constitution is the supreme law of Saint Lucia and, subject to the provisions of Section 41[8] of the Constitution, if any other law is inconsistent with the Constitution it shall prevail and the other law shall, to the extent of the inconsistency is void."**

The Constitution is sublimely sacrosanct and absolute in its majestic constancy. Provisions in the Election Act or any other

---

[8] Section 41 refers to the various modes of amendment to the Constitution.

subsidiary or enabling legislation, if inconsistent with the Constitution, is void.

It is important to note the similarity, in some measure, between Section 35(1) and Section 36(1) of the Constitution. Section 35 is titled SPEAKER and Section 36 is titled DEPUTY SPEAKER. The first twenty-two (22) words of both sections are identical. They read:

"When the House first meets after ant general election of members and before it proceeds to dispatch any other business..."

The significance of these twenty-two (22) words is to establish the temporal template of expediency for what is to follow. "Time" is absolutely of the essence. The House cannot be lackadaisical or complacent. What needs to be done must be done with dispatch. In both instances the whole of subsection (1) is time related; but in their totality there is an order of pragmatic supremacy. If during the course of a parliamentary term the Speaker becomes disabled, the solution reposes within Section 35(1) where it reads:

"The House shall as soon as practicable elect another person to that office."

In Section 36(1) it reads:

"The House shall as soon an convenient elect another member..."

With the disabled Speaker, the House is virtually crippled; but with a disabled Deputy Speaker (however disabled) there is a certain temporal elasticity. And hence, the reason why in one instance there is "as soon as practicable" and in the other "as soon as convenient".

The two terms liberally invoke the principle of *"ejusdem generis"* which makes the effluxion of time regnant, and does not dispense with the presence of a Deputy Speaker at any time or for an inordinate period of time. And since the presence of a Deputy Speaker can be needed at any time during a sitting, logic, parliamentary necessity, efficiency, and continuity dictate that he or she (Deputy Speaker) should be at the ready.

And so "as soon as convenient" is circumscribed by the term readiness and which when operationally and pragmatically translated means at the next or subsequent sitting of the House. And thus a Deputy Speaker, contextually speaking, is elected.

This element of "time" or "when" is further emphasised in Section 3(1) of the Standing Orders, which was made under the CONSTITUTION and approved by the HOUSE on the 14th May 1978. In this section, what is made abundantly clear, and in relation to our present and seeming predicament, the election of the Deputy Speaker is effectuated when it is necessary to so do. As I see it, whenever a Deputy Speaker becomes disabled the election of another Deputy Speaker becomes necessary. And unlike Section 35 of the Constitution where the election of the Speaker is presided over by the Clerk, the election of the Deputy Speaker is presided over by the Speaker of the House.

What then is the House? It is the body of elected members present including the Speaker. And in conformity with the quorum of seven that is needed for government business to be legally transacted then that number must be present.

Though the Speaker presides over the election of the Speaker, it is, and according to convention and custom, the Prime Minister, the first among equals, who carries the election process forward. As is usually the case, the Leader of the Opposition merely responds in his inimitable fashion and in his own deliberate judgement.

As stated in recent times "an appointment made by the House cannot be refused". That is asinine. There is no appointment to be made. Section 36(1) alludes to an election in its contextual significance.

At this time, the question that titillates our thinking iswho will be our next Deputy Leader? Since she has resigned from that position (so I have been told) to direct in some measure a ministerial portfolio the position of Deputy Leader has to be filled. From my knowledge (limited) all elected members on the Government side have been encumbered with a ministerial assignment. And so the question that comes to the fore is who will replace the Honourable Sarah Flood Beaubrun – the former Deputy Leader??

It is not incumbent on the Opposition to extricate the Government from a quandary of its own making.

Who then will be the Sacrificial Lamb?

Whatever the metamorphosis, the Law only constant is Evolution. Our Hope.

THE CREATION OF THE RUDY JOHN BEACH PARK: LABORIE

I am Dr. Velon Leo John who municipally represented the constituency of Laborie for five (5) years informally and fifteen (15) years formally or officially.

During those last fifteen years I was a Parliamentarian with five years as a member of the Opposition and ten years as a Minister of Government.

Please note that the temporal element is not absolute but approximate.

THE PROCESS (1).

One day while officially representing the constituency of Laborie, I decided to walk and explore the full length of the Laborie Bay. That is, from the South (Labatwee) to the North: Cholewa/En Bas Coco.

At the northern end, I saw a portion of land which, in the very distant past, was used as a cemetery for persons who had effected their terrestrial demise as a result to the then raging cholera epidemic, hence the name "cholewa". With the abatement of that plague coconut trees randomly grew in the area.

From these times to the almost present that portion of land was used as a garbage dump and village latrine. The environment was anything but salubrious. But then, as I looked at it I was able to discern certain possibilities. In my mind's eye I saw a community beach if cleared, cleaned, made pristine and functional. I decided to do just that.

THE PROCESS (2).

I requested of my friends, the Daher family of Vieux Fort (Mr. Joe, Mikey, Bryan Charles), to clear and clean that portion of land for me, since they were involved in the heavy equipment business. They acceded to my request and tons and tons of garbage detritus were removed from the site and transported to the Vieux Fort garbage dump. When that was completed, Cholewa/En Bas Coco had metamorphosed into a marine, littoral paradise. Indeed it was a site to behold. Before me was now a beach park with all kinds of functional and salubrious possibilities. When that was done, I asked Mikey to build me a motorable path to the water's edge to facilitate the members of CLUB SIXTY and others to access the warm and placid waters of that portion of the Laborie Bay. That was done.

THE PROCESS (3).

A wooden structure was erected to facilitate vending at the Park and for storage. The next step was to have fourteen picnic tables built for the Park; and in this regard I engaged the Prison authorities. The inmates therein joyfully embarked on that project and constructed the fourteen picnic tables which were painted green. Using the prison truck, the tables were transported to Laborie. The inmates thoroughly enjoyed themselves. If I recall correctly, I was the Minister of Home Affairs at the time.

THE PROCESS (4).

While at the Beach Park it then occurred to me that this Beach Park so pulchritudinous in its appearance should not only be used during the day. The Gods Athena and Bachuus do not sleep. There were nocturnal possibilities, some venereal, recreational and economic. I then contacted my friend, Mr. Sewador, of the Infrastructure Ministry, and who at that time had been assigned to the Electrical Department, and requested of him to provide me with lights for the Beach Park. This he did and so the Beach Park became the first and only lighted Beach Park on the island.

THE PROCESS (5).

With the Beach Park virtually completed I decided to give this beautiful and functional piece of real estate a name. As I saw it, and for historical and other purposes, a Park has to have a name. To be quite candid, I thought of myself, but that went against my sensibilities – against the grain. In my mind, I virtually canvassed the population of Laborie, including Mrs. Agatha Jn Panel after and for whom the Laborie Girls Educational Complex should be named; and that should take place before her mortal existence expires.

THE PROCESS (6).

One Saturday morning while walking along High Street, I saw a certain gentleman walking towards me. As he approached it then dawned upon me that that was the man the Beach Park should be named after. In all respects he personified Laborie: he was a true Laborian, a man of the Lab. I went up to him and told him that I would like to name the Beach Park after him or in his name, as in my opinion he was a fitting person for that honour. Throughout his life he has made Laborie proud. His response was one of bewilderment and reticent. From what I knew of him, one of his sterling qualities was humility. We spoke at some length and then he said, "Brother John, do what you want." I replied, "It is a deal." We shook hands, he smiled and then we parted. That gentleman was none other than RUDY JOHN; affectionately called RJ. To this day, I have never heard anyone objecting to this naming exercise. The Rudy John Beach Park has been accepted by all – here and abroad.

THE PROCESS (7).

I then set a date for the opening or commissioning of the Park. It was a grand opening.

THE RUDY JOHN BEACH PARK was born.

EPILOGUE:

In my opinion, that Park was the crowning achievement in my life as a Minister of Government for since then, and to this time, the RUDY JOHN BEACH PARK has functionally and salubriously impacted on various aspects of the community life of Laborie and also many a Lucian. And in this regard, **Recreation, Tourism, Health and Economics come to mind. The RUDY JOHN BEACH PARK is indeed a national asset.**

Immortality has been conferred on RUDY JOHN and GOOGLE and other platforms evidence the novel geographic representation of LABORIE for all time. To put this request/application into its proper and holistic perspective, I have included a missive addressed to me by one of the icons of Laborie that is, Mr. Watson Louis, and which letter was dated the 7th September 2006 and carbon copied to the then Prime Minister, Dr. Kenny D. Anthony:

P. Watson Louis
Louis Hill
Laborie

Hon. Velon John
Parliamentary Representative – Laborie/Augier

cc Prime Minister Dr. Kenny Anthony

September 7, 2006

Dear Bro. Velon,

Now that you have decided to make your exit as Parliamentary Representative, I take the opportunity to applaud you for what has been unquestionably three terms of good quality representation. Of course, the LAB expected no less from a Laborian. I also wish to applaud the Labour Party government for its overall achievements in only ten years. I applaud you as a friend and a fellow Laborian who is keen on the development of Laborie, and one who also had the privilege of collaborating with you even in a small way in some of the projects. Above all, I have lived in this constituency for the last seventy-two years and I am able to express these sentiments.

Your stewardship was characterized by intelligence, selflessness, wisdom, foresight, loyalty, humility, honesty, hard work, and goodwill to all and sundry — a legacy of noble attributes which future representatives as well as those who aspire to be leaders can emulate.

You inherited a constituency which for most of thirty years prior to 1997, was punished and left neglected by a UWP government because of the pattern of voting of the constituency which did not favor that government. History will record not only your record-breaking three successive election victories and your good work but also the support of a caring, compassionate, and selfless Labour Party Government whose administration has transformed the quality of life of the people of this constituency to a standard consistent with living in civilized times.

In your determination to improve Laborie, you knocked on every door of opportunity — one is reminded of your powerful presentations in Parliament; your many missives to the various government ministers; your personal contacts and on-the-spot visits with ambassadors and other persons; and your appeals for assistance to private business enterprises.

In this regard, the extension of one or more of either pipe-borne water, electricity including street lamps, telephone, or the construction of footpaths in all the thirteen communities of Laborie/Augier, regardless of the size or location of the settlement, is a testament to your efforts.

In some cases, entire communities and in other cases sections of communities are enjoying these facilities for the first time even though these communities have existed from very early times, or as you would remind the nation, "have existed for over one hundred years." This achievement is very significant because these amenities have impacted positively in one way or another on the lives of everyone in those communities. Ma Jomel in particular comes to mind. Your persistent efforts in achieving these demonstrate your genuine desire to improve the welfare of everyone in the constituency.

The transformation of "Cholera" into RUDY JOHN BEACH PARK is a big one for you — it was your idea; you sought and obtained help for the project, creating history in the process; and you single-handedly supervised the works. The Park has become the recreation resort for St. Lucians at large and stands out as the only beach on the island with lights. When the other proposed projects will come on stream, the area will be further enhanced for income-generating activities. By coming up with your choice of name, you did pre-empt attempts to name the Park after you — another sign of your humility — but you made an excellent choice however, because Rudy is another great giant of the LAB. To my mind, the new Community Center should be named "Velon John Administrative Building." I sincerely hope that I succeed in my follow-up work in that regard.

Your dream of the La Battry promenade to complement the new jetty must become a reality in the future — a promenade that should extend from La Battry to the jetty and even beyond to enhance the ambiance of that part of the beachfront for tourism development as envisaged by the Laborie Development Foundation and the Laborie Fishers' and Consumers' Co-operative.

We share any disappointment you may have at not getting certain crucial works attended to — for example, the ravine wall and the bridge to join Eucalyptus Avenue with Louis Hill, the HRDC's, certain road works, Cross Over Field — a general feeling that this constituency did not get the attention befitting its history of support for the Party. But there is some comfort that electricity and pipe-borne water — those two basic amenities — have reached every nook and cranny of the constituency and have indeed changed the daily lives of everyone, particularly the many persons who are enjoying these for the first time.

My family is grateful to you for recognizing us — Ruth for the JP, myself for the OBE. You also gave me the opportunity to serve as Chairman of the Village Council. I wish to note here that Local Councils can be very effective units to help implement government programmes and policies in the various districts if Councils are given the necessary authority.

We wish you good health and God's blessings in the future.

Yours sincerely,

P. Watson Louis

This in some measure attests to the unfolding saga of the Rudy John Beach Park, and further provides an insight into the work accomplished by me in my capacity as a municipal representative for the Laborie Constituency. Further, I also would like it to be noted that the rural electrification of that constituency for the greater part can be attributed to me.

Going a bit further in terms of my public accomplishments I have played a part in the three arms of Government that is, the Executive, the Legislative and the Judiciary.

As regards the Judiciary, I served for about seven (7) years in the Judiciary of the British Virgin Islands and Saint Lucia.

Finally, and for varying periods of time, I have been academically attached to: (1) the University of St. Francis Xavier, Nova Scotia, Canada, (2) the University of Ottawa, Canada, (3) the University of Miami, Florida, USA, (4) the University of Washington, USA, (5) the University of the West Indies, Trinidad (6) the University of Cape Town, South Africa, and (7) the Atlantic International University, Hawaii, USA.

PHOTOS OF ACTUAL MISSIVE

P. Watson Louis
Louis Hill
Laborie.

Hon. Velon John
Parliamentary Representative – Laborie/Augier.

cc Prime Minister Dr. Kenny Anthony.

September 7, 2006

Dear Bro. Velon,

Now that you have decided to make your exit as Parliamentary Representative, I take the opportunity to applaud you for what has been unquestionably three terms of good quality representation. Of course, the LAB expected no less from a Laborian. I also wish to applaud the Labour Party government for its overall achievements in only ten years. I applaud you as a friend and a fellow Laborian who is keen on the development of Laborie, and one who also had the privilege of collaborating with you even in a small way in some of the projects. Above all, I have lived in this constituency for the last seventy two years and I am able to express these sentiments.

Your stewardship was characterized by intelligence, selflessness, wisdom, foresight, loyalty, humility, honesty, hard work, and goodwill to all and sundry - a legacy of noble attributes which future representatives as well as those who aspire to be leaders can emulate.

You inherited a constituency which for most of thirty years prior to 1997, was punished and left neglected by a UWP government because of the pattern of voting of the constituency which did not favour that government. History will record not only your record breaking three successive election victories and your good work but also the support of a caring, compassionate and selfless Labour Party Government whose administration has transformed the quality of life of the people of this constituency to a standard consistent with living in civilized times.

In your determination to improve Laborie, you knocked on every door of opportunity – one is reminded of your powerful presentations in Parliament; your many missives to the various government ministers; your personal contacts and on the spot visits with ambassadors and other persons and your appeals for assistance to private business enterprises.

In this regard, the extension of one or more of either pipe borne water, electricity including street lamps, telephone, or the construction of footpaths in all the thirteen communities of Laborie/Augier regardless of the size or location of the respective community. In some cases, entire communities and in other cases sections of communities are enjoying these facilities for the first time even though these communities have existed from very early times, or as you would remind the nation "have existed for over one hundred years." This achievement is very significant because these amenities have impacted positively in one way or another on the lives of everyone in those communities. Ma Jomel in particular comes to mind. Your persistent efforts in achieving these demonstrate your genuine desire to improve the welfare of everyone in the constituency.

The transformation of "Cholera" into RUDY JOHN BEACH PARK is a big one for you – it was your idea; you sought and obtained help for the project, creating history in the process; and you single handedly supervised the works. The Park has become the recreation resort for St. Lucians at large and stands out as the only beach on the island with lights. When the other proposed projects will come on stream, the area will be further enhanced for income generating activities. By coming up with your choice of name you did pre-empt attempts to name the Park after you – another sign of your humility - but you made an excellent choice however, because Rudy is another great giant of the LAB. To my mind, the new Community Center should be named "Velon John Administrative Building." I sincerely hope that I succeed in my follow-up work in that regard.

Your dream of the La Battry promenade to complement the new jetty must become a reality in the future – a promenade that should extend from La Battry to the jetty and even beyond to enhance the ambience of that part of the beach front for tourism development as envisaged by the Laborie Development Foundation and the Laborie Fishers' and Consumers' Co-operative.

We share any disappointment you may have at not getting certain crucial works attended to - for example, the ravine wall and the bridge to join Eucalyptus Avenue with Louis Hill, The HRDC's, certain road works, Cross Over Field – a general feeling that this constituency did not get the attention befitting its history of support for the Party. But there is some comfort that electricity and pipe borne water – those two basic amenities - have reached every nook and cranny of the constituency and have indeed changed the daily lives of everyone particularly the the many persons who are enjoying these for the first time.

My family is grateful to you for recognizing us - Ruth for the JP, myself for the OBE. You also gave me the opportunity to serve as Chairman of the Village Council. I wish to note here that Local Councils can be very effective units to help implement government programmes and policies in the various districts if Councils are given the necessary authority.

We wish you good health and God's blessings in the future.

Yours sincerely,

THE JOY OF DYING

Having assumed a horizontal posture on my bed of death, I feel very comfortable that the moment of my terrestrial demise is imminent and that the end of my life has arrived.

This comfort springs from the knowledge that I have lived my life, and in the process of so doing have justified my existence. Life as has been said is to be lived and it is an art to live it well: and when that art has passed or is passing you by, then the time has come to graciously and joyously accept the passing of that life.

And one acquires that art not by the doing of great and momentous things but by the sublime expression of your ineffable humanity. And this humanity encompasses the virtues of Love, Compassion, Fairness, Empathy and Fairness. And this sublime expression is another term for doing, and its focus is on persons other than yourself.

By whatever the yardstick, I have lived my life: and now that I am by passing the acquisitive phase of that life, and of which I am very cognisant of, I very rationally can now accept and even embrace the end of this life.

Like all mortals I am flawed, but in the general scheme of things and events, I believe that the positives are greater than the negatives. That provides me with the existential solace / comfort that I need as I contemplate the ebbing away of my life.

As I have indicated I have justified my existence and that yardsticks I have used are (1) I have made my parents proud before their passing (2) I have so positioned my children in such a way and on such a level that they can now deal with the exigencies of their lives and their world and (3) I am satisfied with the impact that I have had on the generalised other. Regardless how minuscule their world, my world is now a better place because I lived. Somebody some where will remember me with a smile: somebody, somewhere will remember me with laughter.

At this point in time the contemplation of death is not morbid nor the reality of my death a tragedy. I am at peace with myself and the world I will leave behind will be a better place because I have impacted upon and on the associates who provided me with the opportunity for the demonstration of Love,Compassion Fairness and Justice in the various and varied spheres of our lives.

What is there beyond my life I do not know. As far as "religion" writ large is concerned, I am in a state of enlightened scepticism. But logically and rationally I hold on to the opinion that homo sapiens as a project is not an exercise in futility. Man is a purpose and has a purpose that in some measure reflects an intelligence that transcends human comprehension and insights.

My level of rationality holds me to the belief that we are not alone in the universe and that there are other dimensions of life that coexist with ours beyond the stars and the galaxies. The virtues of Love, Compassion, Empathy and Fairness are not the product of an arid biosphere or stratosphere but has to be inextricably linked, existentially, metaphysically and ontologically with "being" and "becoming". Homo sapiens falls into the latter category and aspires to the former. Hence the phenomenon of death as the gate-way to the former.

I therefore joyously embrace my death with its eternal salubrious possibilities and to be at one with the quintessence of Creation which as I see it is predicated on a magnificent, celestial Benevolence.

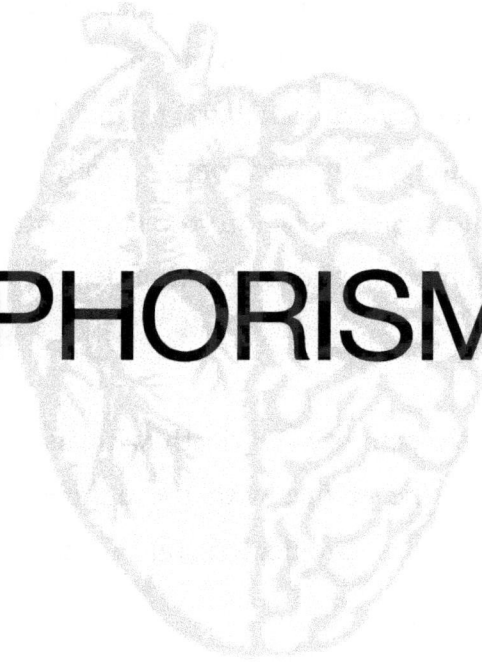

APHORISMS

ALPHA

It is indeed passing strange that the biblical narration of creation does not allude to the complexity, grandeur, majesty and vastness of the universe. What is there reflects the limitation of human knowledge and the limitation at that time with its stupidities and irrationalities: all couched within a cocoon of hope.

ARMAGEDDON

What has been termed "the end of the world" Will not come to pass until the creative Cerebral capacities of man have been Exhausted and with it the inevitable and inexorable quintessential refinement of the moral fibre and life of Homo Sapiens.

BEAUTY

Beauty lies in the mind that contemplates it. And hence its genesis, transmission and expression repose within the essential core of your being. And do all that needs to be done is to open Up yourself to life, and the beauty that is you and of you, will infuse your relational situation with its loving and creative beneficence.

The quintessence of Beauty is of the Soul though it lies in the mind that contemplates.

Let the Truth of your beauty reflect the beauty of your Truth.

Beauty is of the Soul which the Mind transmits across the realm of consciousness, and hence its manifestation is not a function of crass materiality but a cognitive process that has as its genesis the sublimity of that which is Divine.

BEING

In our magnificent humility we ponder on the Bathos and pathos of mortals and wonder Quintessentially as to the ultimate significance of being.

BEING AND NOTHINGNESS

When there is an acute disjunction between "what is" and "what one thought is" then a new reality regardless how morbid or otherwise, comes into existence. The old reality is forever lost as well as that part of oneself that subsisted on "what one thought is".

CAVEAT

Never allow one's actual observational Experience to be lulled into acceptance of one's expectations and over estimations. For the soothing music of one's expectation In the vast majority of instances is but the Jingle of a meretricious melody.

CYNICISM

Horizontal encounters are more fecund Since we have cross fertilisation of ideas Coupled with the rapid conception of an intention.

DECEMBER INTERLUDE

The laughter of love: the sublime joyfulness Of an open family togetherness: the warm glow of a winter's fire and a certain catholic tranquillity. Is this not a glimpse of Heaven as seen through the keyhole of Christmas.

DEATH

Death is the quintessential illusion. It exists by its own demise. It perplexes And intrigues in terms of its beginning and its end It is an epiphenomenon to creation Which is the quintessential state And ultimate expression of becoming. Hence Death is not an end in itself But is a process that leads to a conclusion.

EGO

A scrambler of words
A mad leaper to a star
An unfeathered biped
With a Soul that contradicts
The concoction is Madness.

EXAMS

A cauldron of seething activity Pouring itself on scribbly lines upon the vacant image of one's mind: And conjuring within our cerebral Caves, visions of success and hope. The manna of the fool is hope.

FRIENDSHIP

The Friendship between two men transcends the heterosexual. since the absence of the biological differential purifies the matrix of interaction, sublimates feelings of complementarity and brings to fruition the ideal unity of becoming.

* * *

Your neighbour is that person other than yourself. Embrace her/ him.

HOMO SAPIENS

Man and Woman in their fundamental similarities and differences constitute the two sides of the face of God.

HELL

How can a finite being, in a finite situation, with finite deliberateness, commit a finite act and deserve infinite punishment??

How can a finite being in ninety years of finite existence commit ninety years of misdeeds that are so egregious, so horrific, so morally reprehensible that he deserves infinite punishment.

If that is beyond our finite comprehension therein lies the key – not the answer – to the purpose of human existence.

HUMILITY

Humility is the gate-way to the stars and Love the road-way to the heavens. One leads to the other but they are indivisible. The antidote to the sin of hubris is a sublime HUMILITY.

INTEGRITY

Integrity that is maintained at the expense of the public welfare is anything but integrity. It is essentially intellectual conceit and professional pride: and these two states of mind and attitude are the constitutive elements of the sin of hubris.

INTENTION

Intention is a fool's comfort and paradise: an IMPOSTER if not followed by commensurate action.

JUSTICE

To be a Man and to be just is incompatible. It is Only when he aspires to some principle that Transcends himself, that a notion of Justice Becomes quasi-feasible in operational terms.

KNOWLEDGE

Seduce her, Sophia the goddess of knowledge, and you shall discern the celestial vision of a thousand years.

LAW

As we see it Law should be an agent for social change. But how can this be when most students of Law are ignorant of the social ills endemic in their society. How can we assume a posture of at least redress, when our main concern is the reception of a dubious social accolade and pecuniary gain? Material aggrandisement, meant social status – and this noble concept of Law is relegated to the trash heap of historical and pious oddities.

THE LAWYER

He is essentially a free agent: and it is his intrinsic freedom that gives meaning to the issue of legal ethics. And this meaning is given profound expression in his relationship to the Courts, his client And his community.

In the temple of Justice, he/she is the High Priest or Priestess.

LA VIE

In our productive solitude, we perceive the coming and goings of many feet. They come, they go, they stop. And the frightening realisation is that there is no difference between the stoppings, the comings and goings. A cacophony of sounds: a blur of movement – and the procession of the absurd to the absurd moves along in a circular fashion.

LAUGHTER (1)

Laughter distinguishes Homo Sapiens from that Which is not human. It emanates from the joy of Being and hence it is the sublime nexus with that Which is divine and human. It is an exaltation of the Self however misconstrued and misdirected.

LAUGHTER (2)

To lose one's capacity for laughter is the greatest of tragedies, since laughter is the heart-beat of the Soul and the music of Love. To be unable to laugh is to begin to die.

LIFE (1)

The purpose of Life is living and it is in so doing That the grandest version of your highest self Can be given sublime and exquisite expression.

LIFE (2)

Logic and common sense do not necessarily compliment each other. In human affairs the former must be informed by the latter: but the latter need not be logical since the mind is not the ultimate.

LIFE (3)

The primary law of life is Love: hence self-preservation is anything but the first law of life. For Love is the template upon which a universal altruism can be sustained. And therein lies the salvation of mankind.

LOVE (1)

On whatever the level it is not possible to love that which you do not respect since respect is recognition of your divine genesis.

LOVE (2)

To love yourself you must love that which is love other than yourself since you are of the other.

LOVE (3)

The Supreme and quintessential ACT OF LOVE IS TO FORGIVE THE UNREPENTANT.

MANHOOD

Manhood has never been a consequence of a state attendant to one's chronological status nor masculinity an index of one's carnal peregrinations, which in many instances are mere vapid extensions of a febrile imagination. To be masculine means the honourable expression of one's sexual identity in a situation of social representation. And manhood, the recognition and acceptance of this expression in its multifarious form and modes.

OMEGA

In the final analysis all that matters is tranquillity where the rhythm of Life and the melody of Death are subsumed into one.

POLITICS

The political process is like a roller-coaster. The highs and the lows are inevitable features. The wisdom is to have your highs coincide with critical phases of the process.

* * *

The ultimate virtue and perennial vice of politics is Loyalty.

* * *

Politics is the gateway to the world of hypocrisy, cynicism and malodorous opportunism.

* * *

Politics do not make strange bedfellows. What is evidenced is a debased commonality within the framework of politics and spawns.

* * *

Hypocrisy is the cardinal virtue/vice of politics.

* * *

The Morality of politics is Pragmatism.

* * *

If the national good is the highest principle, then personal integrity is subordinate to it.

REALITY

Galvanised at the desk of our existential situation, we solve our lives nihilistically. On the desert of a dubious eschatology, we have created a mirage of nothingness – the unadulterated quintessence of nihility.

RELIGION

An atavistic propensity, elevated by the fallible intelligence of simian mutants projected into the rarified atmosphere of faith and clothed in an ossified mantle of mystery.

SHE

Never over-estimate or under- estimate what a woman will or will not do. And the commonality of the yardstick to be used is that patently indicated by the ordinary experience of mankind.

TAKE TIME

Take time to Pray, it nourishes the Spirit

Take time to Sleep it invigorates the Mind

Take time to Read it edifies the Intellect

Take time to Work it precedes your Achievement

Take time to Cry it unburdens the Heart

Take time to Play it is a Joy among friends

Take time to Laugh it is the essence of Longevity

Take time to Smile it is the beginning of Friendship

Take time to be Thankful it erases the Debt

Take time to Give it is the source of Wealth

Take time to Forgive it is the highest expression of Love

Take time to be Patient it is the best of Times

Take time to be Humble all of the Time

Take time to Love it is the basis of Forgiveness

Take time to Love for without it we are Nothing and there is Nothing

Take Time to Love it is the Gateway to Paradise.

* * *

The Absolute and quintessential manifestation of Love is to forgive the Unrepentant.

THE BLACKMAN

The Blackman must have faith in the Ultimate goodness and rationality of the community of men, but he must have Faith in himself. He must be able to revel in the pulchritude of his negritude: but above all he must be proud of himself

As a Man.

THE CAUSE

Man is essentially an interior being But he is not the ultimate of that which Is truly interior. What he is and what he Becomes must of necessity be a function of the degree of interiority that he attains. It is regrettable that man on a multiplicity of levels is seen and communicated with so exteriorly. This hinders his intrinsic interior development and is the basis of his particular bigotry, universal madness and confusion.

THE CIRCLE

On a very abstruse level the Alpha, and the Omega are essentially united. Hence Life and Death, living and dying are the Siamese twins of Existence. If we say that they are an essential Unity, then love of life and fear of death are a monstrous contradiction, a travesty of logic and the quintessence of the absurd.

THE FUTURE

That which we create and discover.

THE IDEALIST (1)

To what extent can an Idealist compromise? Essentially he cannot. He might try to attain a pragmatic functional existence but which of necessity create a division within himself. A dualism on the level of self exists and he becomes Schizophrenic. He lives in two worlds and the world that he prefers is that which no longer is.

THE IDEALIST (2)

The more idealistic one is the problematic is One's relationship; for the idealist dreams of what was, a certain innocence, and what could be. But the pragmatist lives in terms of what is; and so meet the concrete exigencies of his situation the idealist is torn about by the wild bulls of contending thoughts and emotions. His only solace is his mind: yet his torture chamber is his heart.

THE MEDIA

Some journalists are specimen of low life, who prowl the stygian darkness of human affairs, searching for worms of sensationalism. Generally, a journalist is a person with a tape-recorder in one hand and a microphone in the other, with no cerebral matter in between.

THE SEARCH

We perhaps know what we are looking for.

We perhaps have seen what we are looking for.

But we have not found what we are looking for.

The course of our search is a rather tortuous one; and perhaps we will have lost, when we have found what we are looking for.

THE SEXES

Gender Equality is a universal imperative and a qualified Divine injunction: since Man and Woman constitute the two sides of the face of God.

YOU

Never deny your own intrinsic magnificence.

Never doubt yourself, your capabilities and abilities.

Never accept the futility of your efforts to transform yourself.

Everyone's disability can be an asset or liability.

Your problem is creating yourself according to the other person's perception, vision and expectation of yourself rather than you, creating yourself in terms of your grandest vision of yourself.

In the eyes of God no one has a disability: no one is a disability.

VICTORY

Since victory is a multifaceted phenomenon, it takes a certain wisdom to decide which battle to lose: the process for so doing calls for a fundamental pragmatism and a sublime humility that are antithetical to the sin of hubris.

WISDOM

To be sane in a world of insanity is insanity. Hence the wisdom of my world is Madness.

WOMAN

What is it that differentiates one from the other?

Man and Woman.

Certainly not their objective and disjunctive sexuality however engineered. But their role in the process of creation, which a posteori links with the metaphysical construct of becoming.

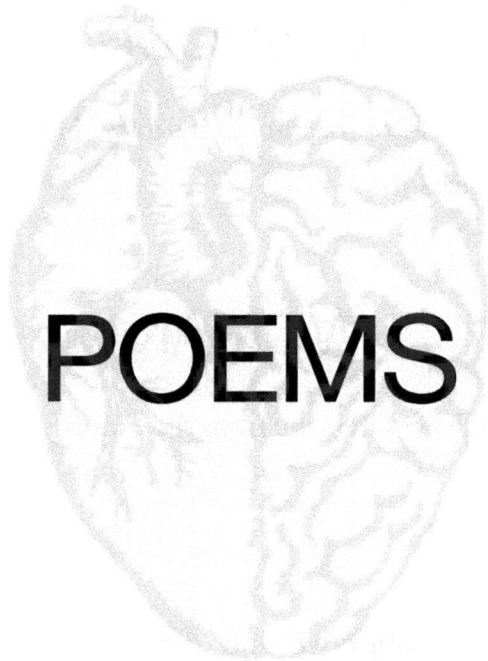

POEMS

LOVING PEACE

Upon enraptured heights she stood
Embracing the presence of his tropical mood
And like a bird with winged expectations
Allowed the night to caress her pulsations.

And he to her face her being was lifted
Till in the dark their presence was sealed
And they like the night their joy was co-founded
As darkness and moon-light commingled their need.

And so from the East the West found its solace
As her laughter of friendship was brought to the fore
And together they left the night to their longing
Consumed and subsumed by love it did bore.

Today the peace of the world is unfolding
As footprints of their path on hearts did explore
And though hate and greed those didn't they follow
The love of their time beyond time did restore.

THE EXISTENTIAL PARADOX

The years pass by in rabid haste
Seeking the present in the futility of the past
With the hope of a future
That is evanescent in its taunting invitation.

And so the that was and is
Nullifies the future that is real
In its unborn innocence
And thus leaving his dreams
Amidst the grains of his thoughts
Sublimely impotent but real.

He then moves along the corridors of his time
Seeking for what he has already found
And thus merging the present with the past
In the hopeful futility of the future.

Unknowingly the Alpha and Omega are united
And time a construct of the mind exists
And thus fulfils the cogito ergo sum of his existence
As the search into and for himself
Perplexes the primary principle of his aetiology.

He thinks therefore he exists

And he is because of his mind

The Alpha and the omega are subsumed into the present

Thus making Life and Death anything but uncertain.

FOR YOU

In Yellow
Thou has attired thy form
A form voluptuous
A form exquisite
But it is they substance
That had adorned my mind
And thus impels me to seek thy hand
Yes, thy hand, thy self, thy form to find.

A DREAM

In her eyes I saw a dream
And it laughing said to me
We are two but one it seems
So what it seems
Let's make it be.

A DIME

When you in waiting spend your time

For time that should be waited

Don't you not wish

A quart or dime to spend

While others dated.

THE CHALICE

A girl she is

And what a girl

Her eyes are brown

And what a brown

Her lips are pink

And what a pink

Her teeth are pearls

What beautiful pearls

Her cheeks are soft

How lovingly soft

A face, her face

All these do form

A countenance

Her countenance of grace is born

How happy is he

For himself should stake

The chalice of her face

And to himself could take.

COMMITTED

I gazed upon thee once tonight
And saw I did I saw a light
Which as my eyes did feast on thee
Awakened me to my heart's decree.

I sat there pondering for a while
Trying to interpret otherwise
But glimpsed I did the sunlight of thy smile
And so I knew it was true not guile

But alas alas, what can I do
For some it seems are committed to
But I will hope though wait in vain
To quench this sweet tormenting pain.

DYING

Though you are away from me
Are upon a distant island
Such the thoughts I conceive you
Such the feelings that overwhelm me
Such the passion that engulfs me
I am dying, dying, dying
Dying to meet you, dying to hold you
Dying to see you, dying to love you,
Will you permit me
Will you deny me
Will you embrace me
Will you accept me
Yes my darling
Will you permit, invite, embrace accept.

SHOULD I

Alone she sits
Alone she thinks
In solemn meditation bent
If I for a while
By her side should sit
Would she in graciousness relent
And for a time in talk assist.

A WINTER'S SUMMER

Across the snow and through the cold
To you my faltering steps were bent
And though with feverish chills
My being quaked
My heart and mind resolved to bear
The cold winds of thy homeland.
Oh Ottawa, oh land of snow
Oh land of cold
In a lover's net you have ensnared me
And though to you I seem to cling
Yet it is her voice
Her charming voice
That within myself doth sing.
Yes, there exists within thy frozen core
Existing there in silent benediction
A jewel of warmth
A jewel of cheer
By her beneficence she has absolved thee
By her presence she has warmed thee
In a blanket
Of Imaginative sunlight.

INDIGNATION

For a brief moment
A truant ray of sunlight
Caressed and kissed
Your dark brown locks
And as it danced
With many a silken strand
My heart rebelled
At this seeming desecration.

THE PEARL

Upon the shores of time she stands
Immaculate in her nakedness
And like a pearl
Beneath a thousand waves of sea
She commands all things
Within her sphere of radiance.
Though delicately created
She reflects in her person
A Samson strength of beauty
Loveliness and grace.
She is a pearl
Amidst a million grains of mortals
Who in majestic simplicity
And with the laughter of the sun
Has enveloped me
In the regal folds of her person.

THE DREAM

Between the sloping mounds of Venus
Lies her gentle loving heart
Speaking in pulsating whispers
To a dream across the seas.

From his perch upon the waters
In expectant mode he waits
As the ripples of her longing
Come adrifting at his feet.

In her clear and innocent waters
Springs the image of his face
Till her form and substance gaping
Grasps him firmly to embrace.

With a frenzied joy she grips him
In abandonment he plunged
Till the dream of their togetherness
In their waters was dissolved.

Thus it was sublime communion
From across two distant lands
She in bed and he in torment
Waiting, waiting to be held.

MADNESS

In an asylum of time I met thee
Dark, mysterious disturbing
An obscure presence
It was madness.

With bolts of thunder
You riveted my attention
And then like silver of mercury
You slithered away in silence.

You gave me
I accepted what you gave
It was nothing
You called
I responded
Yes, I responded to the call
Of my imagination.

Your voice, the voice of madness
Night that voice
And now I hear myself
Me crying for myself
Along the corridors of my existence
It is madness.

Flashing thunder
Midnight laughter
All is dark and mysterious
I am a stranger
Night, night, dark, dark
It is midnight blackness
I see, I see you by the light
Of nothingness illuminated
From the womb of my thoughts
I conceived thee
And with the intensity of my imagination
You were placed in the realm of my orbit.

But then it was all a miscarriage
For you crept from your cradle of love
Crawled to the arms of another
The maddened abortionist.

So it is madness, it is madness
As I laugh and cry at the stars
My heart I claw with my mind
As I watch your ungodly decline
Your delicious perfidy.

THE PARADOX

In a cauldron of seething excitement
In a web of expectation
In a quagmire of anticipation, he sits
Immobilised, impotent, frustrated and castrated.

He shouts his futility of self in whispers
He laughs at the absurdity of his existence
He cries at his inimical proximity to life, to truth.

He is surrounded and immersed in pseudo life, pseudo reality
The excitement is spurious
And the tremulous projections of the beings around
Him
Are indicative of a very concrete mobility.

He is estranged, estranged from himself and the world
Him
Yet estrangement is the key to his life and his death.

In his blindness he sees the world around him
In its myriad forms and shapes
With claws of his mind he grasps at it
At seeming life he grasps and he claws
A painful experience, excruciating joy.

Before him and on the seat of his consciousness
Lies his throbbing tattered heart
The innermost core of his sensibilities, his humanity.

Through the eyes of his desires
He perceives grains of morality
Blowing hither, going thither
But always very still
...Fixed mobility, insane sanity, diabolical
Godliness stultifying freedom and seeing blindness
Grains of sand – a god's insanity.

Going hither blowing thither going, never, ever
Still
It is madness

And so in a shell devoid of substance
In a world devoid of meaning
He stands alone.

In the freezing consciousness of his mind
In the burning awareness of his fate
He stands alone: Alone, a stranger
In the naked prison of his freedom.

THE STRANGER

Alone besides the pool of life
He ponders
Ripples of time flitter by
And yet he ponders
For he is the stranger
Of another time and place
Caught in the webbed wheels
Of his temporal plane.

Ontology denied, teleology askance
He seeks in futile gestures
The thread of life
The thread of truth
Among the pathos of his internal self
Among the bathos of their ingrained conceit.

Along a weary path of life he trods
In search of self
In search of human kind
But there amidst the tangled thorns of man
He sees a petal of a once enchanting flower
Encrusted within
A living tomb of stone.

The seed of life, the seeds of truth
The seeds of beauty and of innocence
All this he seeks
For only in such terms can he belong
Only in such forms
Can he the stranger cease to be.

Groping his way along
His painful night of experience
His anguished soul
Bemoans its earth bound thrust
And yet the stranger
In his absurd hope
Plods on and on
To find a place, with whom.

Alone he stands,
Alone with himself, complete
For he is a stranger
of another time and place
caught in the webbed wheels
of this temporal plane
Hoped for a while
Despite their ingrained deceit.

NOTES

www.ingramcontent.com/pod-product-compliance
Lightning Source LLC
Chambersburg PA
CBHW070118100426
42744CB00010B/1859